IZZARD INK
PUBLISHING

MAKING OF A CHAMPION
The Art of Significant Team Building

**Where Self-Mastery Is Permanent, Winning Is Personal
And High Performance Is Automatic**

BY DAN CLARK
Hall of Fame Speaker
New York Times Best Selling Author
Award Winning Athlete
Championship Winning Coach

"Every Battle Is Won Before It Is Fought"
– Sun Tzu, Art Of War

"Winning is all about preparation. When you know what you are doing and what your opponent's strengths and weaknesses are, once you get into the game the adjustments that you need to make become obvious and simple – not easy, but clear and manageable and doable. You know you are prepared when everybody knows exactly what to do in every situation. Winning is the result of detailed practiced preparation, which creates extreme confidence to execute under pressure."
– Coach Bill Belichick, NFL New England Patriots, Super Bowl Champions

MAKING OF A CHAMPION

The Art of Significant
Team Building

**Where Self-Mastery Is Permanent, Winning Is Personal
And High Performance Is Automatic**

TABLE OF CONTENTS

ACKNOWLEDGEMENTS

For my Coaches who believed in me and molded me into the man I am:

Gene Thompson, Din Morris, Ken Clayton, Tom Thorum, Grant Martin, Ted Weight, Dale Simmons, Vince Zimmer, Tom Gadd, Sam Moore, Ron McBride, Koto, John Pease, Roger Dupaix, and Steve Marshall.

For K.C., Danny, Nikola, McCall, and Alexandrea for finding wisdom, comfort, laughter, learning and solace in my speeches, stories, anecdotes, systems and words. I love you and need each of you in my life forever.

MUST READ INTRODUCTION

In an article published by the learning/training organization "Skills You Need," we get a glimpse into the ever evolving, all-encompassing world of coaching. Put simply, the term 'coaching' means many different things to different people, but is generally about helping individuals to solve their own problems and improve their own performance. Coaching is a process that aims to improve performance and focuses on the 'here and now' rather than on the distant past or future.

While there are many different models of coaching, in this book I am not considering the 'coach as expert' but, instead, the coach as a facilitator of learning.

There is a huge difference between teaching someone and helping them to learn. In coaching, fundamentally, the coach is helping the individual to improve their own performance: in other words, helping them to learn. Good coaches believe that the individual always has the answer to their own problems but understands that they may need help to find the answer. Coaching is unlocking a person's potential to maximize their own performance. It is helping them to learn rather than teaching them.

THE 'INNER GAME'

Timothy Gallwey's book, The Inner Game of Tennis, revolutionized thinking about coaching. He suggested that the biggest obstacles to success and achieving potential were internal, not external. His insight was that coaches could help individuals to improve their game by distracting them from their inner dialogue and, in particular, the critical voice that said "Not like that! Concentrate on your hands! Angle it differently!"

By distracting that inner voice, the body could take over. It turns out that often the body has a very clear idea of what to do when internal dialogues are suppressed. Gallwey used the example of asking people to focus on the height at which they hit the tennis ball. This activity has no relevance in itself, but the simple act of focusing on it distracted the inner voice and enabled the capable body to take over. The individual relaxed and their tennis improved immediately.

Gallwey's real insight was that this didn't just apply to tennis, but that individuals generally did have the answers to their own problems within themselves.

The essential part of coaching, then, is to help people to learn to silence that inner voice and allow their instincts, or their subconscious, to take over. Sometimes that means distracting it, and sometimes it's about exploring the 'worst case scenario' and removing the fear.

Coaches need to identify the stage at which an individual is at to use the right sort of language to help them move to the next stage. After all, it's difficult to try to improve a skill if you don't know that you lack it.

THE DIFFERENCES BETWEEN TEACHING, COACHING, MENTORING AND COUNSELING

Although Teaching, Coaching, Mentoring and Counseling all share some key characteristics and skills, they are nonetheless quite different and it's important to be aware of the differences.

TEACHING AND TRAINING

Teaching and training involve an expert teacher who imparts knowledge to their students. Although the best teachers will use participative and interactive techniques, like coaching, there is very definitely an imbalance of knowledge, with the teacher as expert knowing the 'right answer'.

COACHING

Coaching involves the belief that the individual has the answers to their own problems within them.

The coach is not a subject expert, but rather is focused on helping the individual to unlock their own potential. The focus is very much on the individual and what is inside their head. A coach is not necessarily a designated individual: anyone can take a coaching approach with others, whether peers, subordinates or superiors. The key skill of coaching is asking the right questions to help the individual work through their own issues.

MENTORING

Mentoring is similar to coaching. There is general agreement that a mentor is a guide who helps someone to learn or develop faster than they might do alone.

In the workplace mentors are often formally designated as such by mutual agreement, and outside of an individual's line management chain. They usually have considerable experience and expertise in the individual's line of business. A Mentoring relationship usually focuses on the future, career development, and broadening an individual's horizons, unlike coaching which tends to focus more on the here and now and solving immediate problems or issues.

Counseling is closer to a therapeutic intervention. It focuses on the past, helping the individual to overcome barriers and issues from their past and move on. Here, the focus may be either internal or external. The differences between these various 'learning methods' can be summarized based on the work of: Clutterbuck, D. & Schneider, S. (1998):

Learning Method:	Coaching	Mentoring	Counseling
The Question:	How?	What?	Why?
The Focus:	The present	The future	The past
Aim:	Improving skills	Developing & committing to goals	Overcoming psychological barriers
Objective:	Raising competence	Opening horizons	Building self-understanding

It doesn't matter whether coaching is used in sport, life or business, the good coach believes that individuals always have the answer to their own problems. They just need help to unlock them.

CHAPTER ONE

SETTING EXPECTATIONS

"You can't coach results, you can only coach behavior by redefining what's possible with attitude and expectations"
—Dan Clark

MAKE IT REAL

A classic example of the power that comes from setting high expectations occurred a few years ago when a former professional baseball player moved into my brother's neighborhood in California. His name was Rob. He was not married and had no children. When my brother and a group of parents approached him about coaching their eight-year-old sons' Little League baseball team, Rob accepted the challenge. One week later he called a mandatory meeting for all parents of the participating players.

Rob made each parent sign a contract he had drawn up by his attorney that guaranteed they would never yell at the umpires, that they would never say anything derogatory to any player or coach or parent on any team, and that they fully comprehended the fact that 8-year-olds would not be playing in the World Series, so they should lighten up and let the kids have fun. Rob made sure each parent realized that Little League was not the place for parents to live out their frustrated, unfulfilled, broken childhood dreams through their children, and that he would expect more from the parents and their sons.

MAKE IT CHALLENGING

My brother's son Joshua was excited to play and ran home from his first practice to show his dad an exact-size cardboard replica of home plate that coach Rob had given to him. Joshua put the plate on the kitchen floor with the point facing backward, got in his batting stance and excitedly started to explain:

"Dad, Coach Rob made one of these for each player on the team. Coach said hitting is about balance and bat speed, and so to make sure I'm not too far forward or too far backward, I need to put my belly button right even with the first corner point on home plate. Coach said that to hit the ball, my left foot heel should be off the ground as if it were resting on an egg.

"And when I swing the bat, I need to slightly stride forward with my left foot, smash the egg with my heel, and twist my hips and back foot around as if I was squishing a bug. Dad, I can hit the heck out of the ball if I just stand up there, keep my head still, smash the egg, and squish the bug. See, Dad, it's all written down on this paper that my coach gave me! And Coach Rob said to get you to help me practice smashing the egg and squishing the bug 100 times tonight and every night before I go to bed!"

MAKE IT FUN

I was a pretty good baseball player as a division one university student athlete and I didn't learn this much about hitting until I was nineteen years old and playing college ball. Joshua was eight! And how did Coach Rob teach his players to slide properly? Most coaches take their players to the ball field and have them get in a line between third base and home plate, and run and slide on the hard cement-like dirt that tears their pants and skin, which makes them afraid to do it in a game when it counts.

Coach Rob took his boys to a grassy hill where he instructed them on the proper way to bend their leg and where to put their hands in a picture perfect slide position. Then, with a water hose, he soaked the grass and had the boys get a running start and slide to see who could go the farthest! His players never wanted to stop practicing!

And how did Rob teach his players to hit the "cut- off-man" when throwing the ball in from the outfield? Other coaches would just yell "throw it in to the shortstop." Rob got a mannequin and dressed it up like a goofy rock star. He staked it into the ground by second base and had the boys catch a fly ball and then turn and try to knock over the mannequin. Those who did got ice cream, and the team stayed at practice until every kid hit it!

MAKE IT SIGNIFICANT

Weeks later, the anticipation of using all they had learned was finally over as the players arrived at the ballpark and the bleachers filled up with parents and friends from both teams for little Joshua's first big game. It was also Rob's first game as a coach, and he had arrived two hours earlier to get everything ready.

By the time everybody arrived, Rob had raked and weeded the infield and had borrowed the machine from the San

Francisco Giants organization to line the field and batters box. There was no sound system at the park, so Rob purchased 350 feet of electrical extension cord. He had plugged it into a backyard outlet, stringing it through a field along a sidewalk and into the park, where he had it plugged into a boom box next to an 8-foot flagpole he had pounded into the ground with a beautiful American flag waving in the breeze.

To begin the game, Rob held a megaphone up to his mouth and invited everyone to stand for the national anthem. His entire team of fifteen 8-year- old boys followed Joshua out of the dugout in single file. They lined up on the third-base line, turned to face the flag, stood at attention, simultaneously took off their hats, and placed them over their hearts.

Rob then put the megaphone down by the boom box to amplify the sound, pushed play on the CD player, and joined his team in loudly and proudly singing the "Star-Spangled Banner!" Parents and the other team players and coaches were amazed and pleasantly surprised as they quickly joined in.

'OWN IT' AND MAKE IT PERSONAL

To no one's surprise, every kid on Joshua's team hit the ball every time they came up to bat and were having the time of their lives, while most of the players on the other team could not swing the bat properly, could not hit the ball, and were not having fun.

The other team's expectations were low, resulting in a minimum effort, mediocre complacency, with the parents and coaches yelling at the umpire and making excuses for their children's poor performance.

Coach Rob's expectations were not short- term. He had long-term, big-picture results in mind, knowing that the most important thing in coaching youth is to help them get pretty good at the fundamentals, make sure they have fun, play by the rules, demonstrate respect and sportsmanship, and instill a true love for the game. Not just for players, but for fans!

Up until this first game, the ballpark had never had a concession stand. So Coach Rob had also organized someone to sell hot dogs, peanuts, and soft drinks. Little League games only go six innings, so there is no opportunity to break for a traditional seventh inning stretch and a rendition of "Take Me Out to the Ball Game" like they do in the major leagues.

Consequently, Coach Rob had everyone break for a three-inning stretch and led the entire park in the fabled tune. "It's not a real baseball game without dogs, nuts, drinks, and an attempt at the ball game song," Rob said after the game. The team went on to win the league championship. The boys are now over 25 years old and have never forgotten that season.

Question: did what they learn from Coach Rob teach them skills and work ethic and values that continue to mold their minds and fuel their passion for personal greatness? Absolutely! The power of Setting High Expectations is timeless and immeasurable!

MAKE IT REWARDING

With some of these young players who were now adults in the audience of a fundraising gala that I was hosting, Major League Baseball Hall of Fame superstar Cal Ripken Jr. was asked by a ten year old boy when he decided he wanted to be "Iron Man" and break Lou Gehrig's (1903-1941) record of 2,131 consecutive games played without any interruption. Cal smiled and answered, "I never even knew the record existed until I got close to breaking it and the media made a big deal about it. I never set out to break any record. I just loved the game of baseball so much that I couldn't wait to practice every day and play in every game! The record just took care of itself! As they say, 'When you love what you do, you never work a day in your life.'

Because Ripken loved the journey and made it meaningful, ending up at a meaningful destination was a predictable reward. Consequently, the perseverance, endurance and everyday work ethic that Ripken exhibited throughout his twenty-one seasons with the Baltimore Orioles made him one of the most popular professional athletes in all of sports.

MAKE IT CONSISTENT

If you have played or coached Little League Baseball you will know that Home Plate is 17 inches wide. How wide is Home Plate in Babe Ruth League? 17 inches. How wide is Home Plate in high school and college baseball? 17 inches. How about in the pros? It is 17 inches wide! Regardless if you have a pitcher on the team who can throw it 100 mph, if he doesn't throw it over the plate somewhere within the 17 inches for a strike, he won't play much.

It doesn't matter how old he is, or if he is the coach's son, or if he is the best player in the league, or how long and loud he whines and complains, no one in the league is going to widen Home Plate to 19 inches or 25 inches just to accommodate a pitcher who can not rise to the occasion and meet the high expectation standards set by the league. No Exceptions! Period.

If your best player on your team comes late to practice or is caught drinking or breaking curfew before a game or grows facial hair when it's against team policy, will you 'bend' the rules and 'widen' Home Plate and enlarge the strike zone because he is your 'franchise superstar'? Or will you stay strong and consistent and suspend him like you would any other player?

Championship winning coaches who master the Art of Significant Team Building teach their players the never changing rules of the game, establish high expectations for their players to obey the rules, hold them accountable with both rewards for following the rules and consequences for not following the rules, and never widen the plate. The hard truth is if you are a pitcher who can't consistently throw the ball over Home Plate for a strike, you either sit the bench or change positions to use your other skills to do something equally important to help the team win! And if you can't throw or hit or catch or run, you find a different sport – you play a different game - no shame!

MAKE IT HARD AND WORTH IT

The purpose and mission of a parent is to prepare our children for a world they recognize. The real 'free market,' incentive-motivated world in which everybody is required to compete and live. If there is only one job offer and nine applicants, who is going to get the job? The obvious answer must be 'the one who is most qualified regardless of race, ethnicity, creed, gender or socioeconomic status.'

The purpose of the Olympic Games is to invite world class athletes to compete in front of millions of people to see who is the fastest, who can go farthest, who is the strongest, who can jump highest and who can score the most points on that particular day. The Olympics are a showcase of extraordinary human beings who have accumulated thousands of hours of practice and years of sacrifice and hard work just for the privilege to perform for 2 minutes in an event or for 60 minutes in a game, for a chance to win a Gold or Silver or Bronze medal.

What would happen to the Olympic Games if every competitor won the same Gold Medal no matter what their score was or how they finished in the competition? If we stopped keeping score would world records ever be broken, or would we ever see an athlete dig deep inside to find the 'second wind' to hustle and somehow give it that 'something more' to achieve greatness? If every competitor received the same 'participation trophy' and got the same 't-shirt' for just showing up, would we ever see anyone rise above the minimum requirement average mediocrity that low achievers want to establish as the norm for everybody else?

CHAPTER TWO

STRETCHING EXPECTATIONS

"Not every football play is designed to score a touchdown. If you are getting beat by 20, there are no 20-point plays. It's one play, one yard, one first down, one two point safety, one three point field goal, or one six point touchdown play at a time."
— *Dan Clark*

You may think that stretch, being internally driven, is a solitary process. Not true! Although deciding to stretch is a personal decision, we can stretch ourselves only so far on our own; in order to reach our ultimate capacity and potential as human beings, we need help. Once I snapped my Achilles tendon playing basketball with the guys on my street. My ankle required surgery, and I was put in a plaster cast for three months. To fully recover, I underwent four weeks of physical therapy.

In each session, the first thing the therapist did was warm up my stiff, weakened ankle. Then she took the tip of my foot and bent it and stretched it to a place it had never been. As I gritted my teeth and reminded myself that pain is temporary but quitting lasts forever, she then let go, and my foot flipped back to the same place it was before she started to stretch it. Isn't this the usual outcome of company sales rallies and corporate training where we get pumped up, but then leave and flip on back to the same old attitude and behavior we brought to the meeting?

Stretching requires that someone not merely take us past the point of discomfort, but support us as we hold ourselves in a zone of discomfort so that we can strengthen ourselves. Consider the Vertical Stretching Scale on the next page. Obviously, the first step is to start where we are. Next, we push and strain ourselves to the point of discomfort. Third, we ask someone we trust and respect to stretch us past the point of discomfort and support us there until the strain and stretch are no longer stressful. Once we have grown comfortable at the 7, 8, or 9 levels, those become our new starting points, the new normal, and on our revised, amped- up scale we start again at 1. Now the level that used to be 10 becomes level 6 – no longer the snapping point, but instead the targeted point of discomfort – which we now can handle and surpass with support.

Too many of us want to stretch and strengthen all at once. Leaders set outrageously high, unrealistic goals without giving even a modest amount of support. Then they blame their people when they snap and fall. I know a lot of superstar athletes, corporate executives, military leaders, and professionals in every field who will verify that all strengthening occurs in the area past the point of discomfort. While you can get to the point of discomfort on your own, you need someone else whom you admire and respect to push you past discomfort and then support you there while you strengthen. If you're a manager, now is the time to ask yourself just what are you demanding of your people. Do they realistically have what they need from you to grow? Or are you just setting them up to snap right back to where they were the minute you, as the "physical therapist," stop exerting pressure?

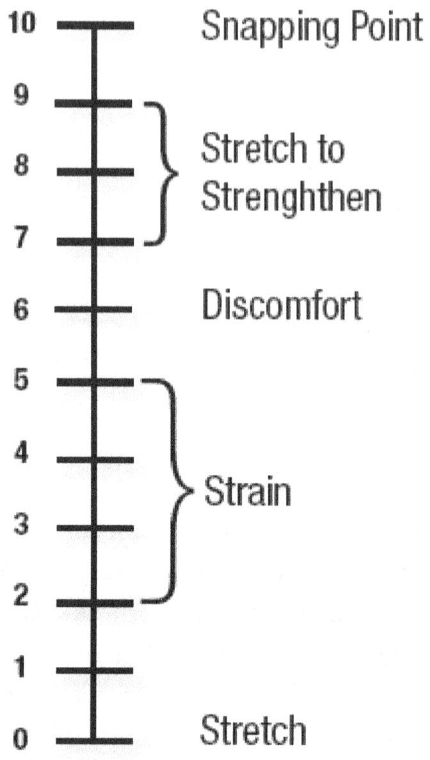

THE BROOMSTICK TEST

A great illustration of the kind of support we need in order to stretch is what I call the "Broomstick Test." When I work with professional or amateur athletic teams, I'll often assemble the team in their meeting room and ask a captain and an assistant coach to come to the front of the room and hold the ends of a broomstick so it is suspended twelve inches off the floor. Ahead of time, I get the name of the premier stud athlete on the team (the one with the thirty-eight- inch vertical leap), and when the broomstick is in place, I ask him to come forward and jump over the bar. I usually find him sitting in the back of the room, and he always hesitates and gives me a cocky, arrogant look, like, Hey, don't you read the newspaper? Don't you know who I am? Why are you bugging me?

After some prodding, he finally strolls up to the front of the room, walking with a swag that looks as though he had sat on something hot. I then ask him if he thinks he can jump over the twelve-inch high broomstick. After he glares at me, conveying that this is a waste of his precious time and how dare I insult his athletic sophistication I ask point- blank, "Will you jump over the broomstick?" Grinning sarcastically, he skips over it and stares me down again.

In front of everyone, I then ask why he only jumped twelve inches high when he and his coaches and teammates know he can jump thirty- eight inches high. Every time I have conducted this exercise in the National Football League, in the NCAA, or in a corporate business retreat, the player or employee has replied, "Because that is all you asked me to do."

This star player is one of the best athletes in the sport, and yet because of his contract, management often can't ask him to give more, do more, be more, or "jump higher." In business, we can't offer a raise every time we want someone to take his or her productivity to the next level. We can't motivate military or political leaders to increase their performance with money or recognition, either. We can motivate them to continue down the road toward significance only by expressing expectations – and not just any expectations, but expectations pegged to their own noble quest, their dream, their purpose.

What are your current expectations in the physical, mental, spiritual, emotional, social, financial, familial and charitable sides of your life? How high is your bar compared to your potential? Who is stretching you? Because all the strengthening occurs in the area past the point of discomfort, and none of us can stretch ourselves to our ultimate capacity as human beings all by ourselves, we all need someone to raise our bar and, most important, to ask us to jump!

We also must dedicate ourselves to going above and beyond the right now – even if we're afraid or otherwise resistant. Obviously we can't jump higher than we are currently able, but still we must keep jumping. If you want to get better at doing pushups, you get better and stronger by doing push-ups. It's easier to act our way into positive thinking than to think our way into positive action. Self-esteem, desire, and motivation are not required to change behavior. We need to change what we're doing – behavior changes behavior!

When do most people fix their health problems? When it's too late. When do most people read a book on relationships? When their relationships are falling apart. We don't need to feel motivated to do motivated! It is not enough for us to be empathetic; we must do empathetic. It's not enough for our company to be customer-centric; we must do extraordinary customer service. We can't just be trustworthy, loyal, helpful, friendly, courteous, kind, obedient, cheerful, thrifty, brave, clean, reverent, unconditionally loving, and forgiving; we must do them!

It's not enough for us to be successful – we must do significance! Because stretching entails a process of bringing change out from within, stretching implies a specific kind of competitive spirit. Successful individuals compete with others, measuring their success against what others accomplish. Significant individuals move along the growth path and attain both material and spiritual greatness by competing against themselves.

Let me ask you: When you assess your own progress and growth, do you compare yourself to your neighbor down the street and the guy in the next cubicle? Or do you measure yourself against your dreams, your purpose, and the principles you yourself hold dear?

When it comes to converting 'change' into 'stretch' remember three things: the Law of Attraction is always in play and states, 'you attract what you believe you deserve; the Art of Significance allows you to Achieve The Level Beyond Success and not just get what you want, but actually want what you get so you don't die with your music still in you. When you come to grips with the reality that no matter where you go, there you are; a mere geographic relocation doesn't change much of anything; you will plainly see the significance of the following self-administered audit that will kick-start your transformational process.

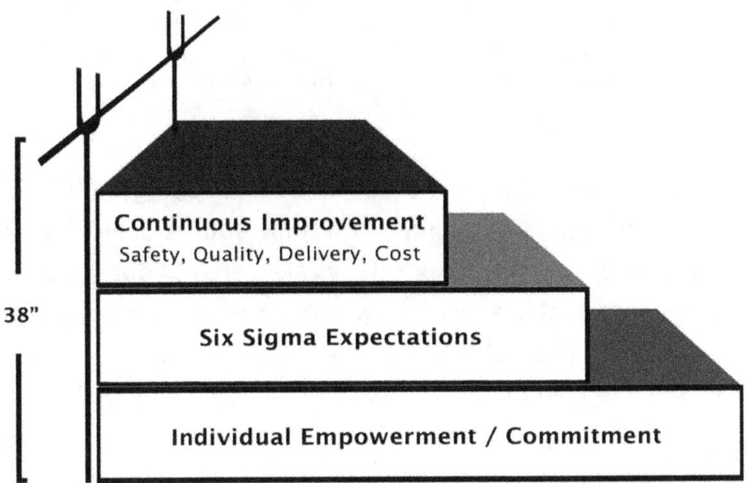

STRETCHING ACTIVITY

Evaluate this "Balance Wheel" diagram combining nine aspects and areas of our lives:

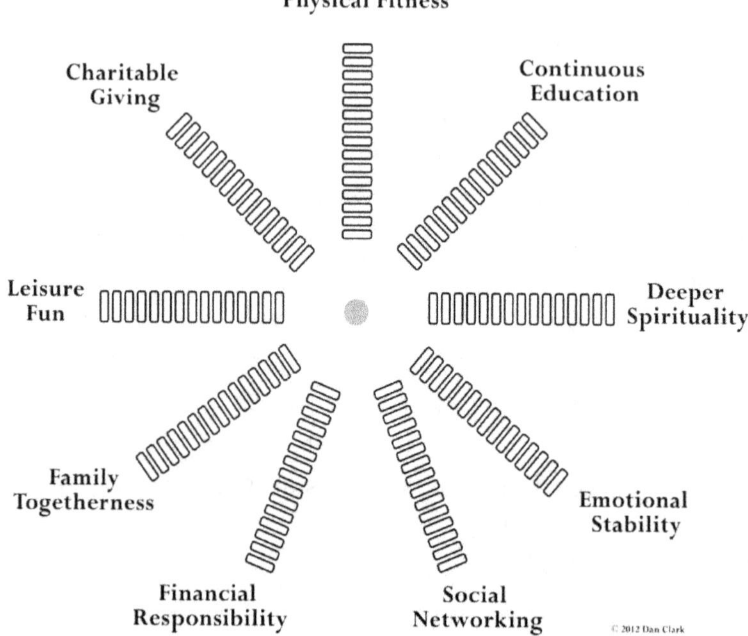

Rating yourself on a scale of 1 to 15 (15 being the highest level of performance), ponder how fully you've been living in the nine areas. Do you purposefully take care of your body? Do your keep your mind active? How fully have you been nurturing your soul with charitable deeds? Do you experience on a daily basis the vital emotions of fear, pain, joy, love, peace and satisfaction? Do you approach your work with an eye toward always learning something new? Because no other success can compensate for failure in the home, and quantity time has a quality all of its own, can your family see that they are the most important thing in the world to you?

Mark the boxes that reflect how you feel you are currently performing, and draw a line to connect your number on the scale with each of the nine categories. This "wheel" is now a snapshot of your life in or out of balance. Which parts of your life are working best right now: body, mind, spirit, emotions, friends, family, career, or finances? Where can you improve – not all at once, but one box, one day, one quality, one attribute, one task at a time?

Remember, when our lives get tough and our ride seems rough and bumpy, most blame the road, when in reality, it is our selves we need to fix. Once we balance and round out our "wheel," the ride is smooth and the way is rewarding.

"PHYSICAL FITNESS"

When deciding to improve your Physical Fitness, the answer comes from two major questions: "Are you physically strong enough to do your required work that is expected in your job description?" And, are you physically fit and cardiovascular strong enough to rise to the occasion in an emergency as a mom, or dad, friend, and neighbor?"

When my youngest daughter was 14 years old she competed as a dancer in ballroom, jazz, tap, contemporary and hip-hop competitions around the country. During an event in Denver Colorado, when she was with her mother and a fellow dance studio member with his mother, I received a frantic phone call from the young man's younger 12-year old brother.

In a terrified voice he explained that his dad – who for the record was a big, strong, solid, 6 foot tall, 200 pound firefighter, had fallen over on the kitchen floor, and was struggling to breathe with his eyes rolling back in his head. The young boy had called 911, and had called his mom in Denver, who told him to call the neighbor lady, and to call me so I could meet them at the hospital, which was 90 minutes from my home.

I hung up the phone and raced in my car to get there as fast as I could. When I arrived, they still had not arrived, and the hospital was only fifteen minutes from their house. What could have gone wrong?

When they finally got to the emergency room, dad was diagnosed as having had a stroke, but had been without oxygen and the proper stroke medication for so long that there was little they could do to help him. And this amazing father, husband, public servant and friend, died.

Was it hospital malpractice? No! When the ambulance showed up dispatched by the 911 operator, the two EMTs were big, over weight, out of shape, weak and heavy breathing men who didn't have the physical strength to lift dad off the kitchen floor and put him on the gurney to roll him into the ambulance and transport him to the hospital. So he laid on the kitchen floor for an hour until they could dispatch a second ambulance with a different qualified and physically fit crew!

At the funeral there were tears of sadness mixed with feelings of anger, all because two EMT's didn't take their physical fitness seriously!

CONTINUOUS EDUCATION

*"Formal education will make you a living.
Self-education will make you a fortune!"* —Jim Rohn

The average American car owner drives between 12,000 and 25,000 miles a year. This translates into 500 to 1,000 hours each year, or the equivalent of 12 to 25 forty-hour work weeks. When you listen to programs in your car you can gain the equivalent of three years of college education in four years' time. Listening to a 90-minute recorded speech is equivalent to reading 40 pages of a book, which is the equivalent of reading a 250-page book every week, which equates to reading 52 books a year or 520 books in 10 years!

List one thing you can do today/tomorrow to improve your score in each of the nine areas of life. Name one person who can/will help you and hold you accountable to work on this one thing every day:

Physical Fitness:

____

____

____

____

Continuous Education:

____

____

____

____

Deeper Spirituality:

____

____

____

____

Emotional Stability:

____

____

____

____

Social Networking:

____

____

____

____

Financial Responsibility:

____

____

____

____

Family Togetherness:

____

____

____

____

Leisure Fun:

____

____

____

____

Charitable Giving:

____

____

____

____

CHAPTER THREE

THE POWER OF 'WHY'

"If you're not failing a few times it means you're not pushing yourself hard enough!" – Dan Clark

I played American football for thirteen years and coming out of the University of Utah I was a projected #1 draft choice by the National Football League Oakland Raiders confirmed in a personal letter from owner Al Davis and his head of player personnel Ron Wolfe. However, one day in practice my lifelong dream of being an NFL star came to a devastating halt.

In a tackling drill the coach whistled, "go," and another player and I ran full speed into each other. After a brutal head-on collision, I lay on the ground in shock, with a sharp, piercing pain shooting through my body. My eye drooped and my speech slurred (which momentarily returned). In one hit I had compressed my neck, severed the axillary nerve in my right deltoid, and suffered a grade-2 concussion.

By nightfall my neck was stiff, my right side was paralyzed, my arm dangled at my side, and I perspired profusely, shook, and threw up until I cried myself to sleep. For the next fourteen months I was paralyzed—both physically and emotionally. My heart was broken, my dreams were shattered, and my successful and promising life came crashing down.

Over the fourteen months I went to sixteen different doctors, all of whom had a different solution to the same diagnosis. Fifteen of the physicians said I only had a 10% chance of recovering and that I would never get any better. Yet, it was this pessimism (they called probability) that motivated me to keep searching until I found a doctor who believed I could get better. His name is Dr. Brent Pratley, who simply replaced 'probability' with 'possibility' and believed that with the right mindset, work ethic and therapy I would get better!

Now that I've recovered I'm often asked what took so long? May I ask you the same question? If you are going to improve and get better, what is holding you back and taking so long?

The answer for all of us is twofold and the same: First I confused who I was with what I did. Do you? I thought I was a football player when in reality that's just what I did, not who I am. When we identify ourselves in terms of what we do instead of who we are, we become human 'doings' instead of human 'beings' – unacceptable if success and a life of significance is what we really seek.

Second: I was asking the wrong questions. I was asking the doctors how to get better when I should have been asking myself, "Why?" As soon as I answered the "why" and felt the "want," figuring out the "what" and "how to" became clear and simple.

Once I stopped focusing on having fame and chasing fortune and started focusing on achieving my real purpose and becoming whole, I was able to persevere the pain of rehabilitation and do the hard things required to become everything I was really born to be.

RESILIENCY AND ADAPTING TO CHANGE

A clearly defined 'why' coupled with a compelling 'want' (goal) have a gigantic impact on behavior because they engage more than simply the brain. They also engage the heart. Research proves that a clear, concise, personally meaningful and challenging goal causes our blood to pump more rapidly, our brain to fire, and our muscles to engage. When I have only a 'what' and a 'how' without a 'why' and a 'want', no such effects take place.

I must know 'why' I do what I do because I can't motivate myself and inspire others with just what I do. I must be able to articulate why I exist and the purpose of every task I am asked to perform. Why is the source of my ambition and motivation and the emotional fuel that drives me to want to achieve personal greatness and push myself to my ultimate capacity and potential as a human being.

When my 'why' became my own, it put focus on my journey and illuminated the fact that when my why is bigger than my why not, I have the personal courage and commitment required to be resilient and adapt to change. However, for my why to survive, it needs the structure of what and how and a destination of where and when, which means I must also "keep" the end in mind.

When an organization has a clearly defined 'why, what, how, where and when,' each team member becomes his and her own motivational speaker, equipped with the ability and confidence to make a decision as clearly and as accurately as the leader/coach. The organizational what and how-to will improve as they magnify the why. Magnifying your why comes through passion, generated when you make your motivation for doing extremely personal and your motivation for persevering extremely profound.

LESSONS LEARNED

Since my injury and subsequent recovery I have interviewed many of the most successful championship winning coaches in both professional football and in NCAA football. Every one of them agrees that winning or losing a game boils down to only six plays. In a typical 60-minute game the two teams compete against each other, either on offense or defense, in only 60 plays. Obviously no one knows at the beginning of the game which will matter most. Nor does anyone know at half time.

Calculating the positive or negative ramifications of each play to determine its impact on the score can only occur when the coaches can assemble in their offices to watch the game film and evaluate which of the plays qualified as one of the six that changed the outcome of the game.

Bottom line. No one – not a player or a coach, can ever take off a play! We must play every play as if it were the last play we will ever play. In my situation it was. Do you remember what happened in the 2017 National NCAA Football Championship Game between Alabama and Georgia? At the end of the game the score was tied, which threw it into overtime.

In the mix of all the excitement, a super star defensive back for Georgia, who had played an outstanding game and had not taken off one play, suddenly lost his focus and energy and forgot his personal 'why,' and let down long enough for an Alabama receiver to easily slide behind him and catch a 41-yard touchdown pass to win the game. Because he took one play off he let himself and his teammates down and Alabama was crowned National Champions. Every play matters! Every player on every play matters!

Based on this understanding, and through my rehabilitation process in recovering from my injury, I realized:

- Adversity introduces us to ourselves and either makes us bitter or better.
- No one will ever know how strong we are until being strong is our only choice.
- No one ever knows what we are really made of until we are squeezed and we can see the quality of the juice that comes out: positively sweet or negatively sour.

- Not every play is designed to score a touchdown. Yet every play has equal value and contributes to winning.
- Momentum is only as good as your next play.
- You can't always control what happens, but you can always control what happens next.
- There is nothing more insignificant than the half time score.
- Get knocked down seven times get back up eight.
- It's not what happens to you that makes or breaks you it's what you do with what happens to you that defines who you are.
- Losing hurts worse than winning feels good.
- When we do today what others won't, we will accomplish tomorrow what others can't, turn our stumbling blocks into stepping stones, and transform our setbacks into come backs.
- Clearly, I am the man I am and have the perspective on life that I live by because of this paralyzing football ordeal.

CHAPTER FOUR

UNDERSTANDING MOTIVATION

"Cripple him, and you have a Sir Walter Scott. Lock him in a prison cell, and you have a John Bunyan. Bury him in the snows of Valley Forge, and you have a George Washington. Raise him in abject poverty and you have an Abraham Lincoln. Strike him down with infantile paralysis, and he becomes Franklin Roosevelt. Burn him so severely that the doctors say he'll never walk again, and you have a Glenn Cunningham who set the world's one-mile record in 1934. Deafen him and you have a Ludwig von Beethoven. Have him or her born black in a society filled with racial discrimination, and you have a Booker T. Washington, a Marian Anderson, a George Washington Carver, and a Martin Luther King Jr. Call him a slow learner, 'retarded,' and write him off as uneducable, and you have an Albert Einstein."

Identifying our 'Why' is a deeper explanation of "Motivation," which is the #1 reason why an individual or a team succeeds or fails, wins or loses. It predicts success better than intelligence, ability, gender, body type, salary and socioeconomic situation.

In everyday usage, the term motivation is frequently used to describe 'why' a person does something. Motivation is the reason for people's actions, willingness and goals. Motivation is derived from the word 'motive,' which is defined as "a need that requires satisfaction through completion the process that initiates, guides, and maintains goal-oriented behaviors."

Motivation is one's direction to behavior, or what causes a person to want to repeat a behavior. Mastering motivation to allow sustained and deliberate repeated behavior is central to high levels of achievement, as in the worlds of elite sport, medicine or music.

Motivation is what causes you to act, whether it is getting a glass of water to reduce thirst or reading a book to gain knowledge or pushing yourself beyond your current performance to get bigger, faster, stronger in an exercise/weight room or perfect your execution in a practice in order to gain the competitive advantage in a game.

BIOLOGY OF MOTIVATION

Motivation involves the biological, emotional, social and cognitive forces that activate, direct, and sustain goal-directed behavior.

Motivation refers to factors that Motives are the 'whys' of behavior—the needs or wants that drive behavior and explain what we do. We don't actually observe a motive. Rather, we infer that one exists based on the behavior we observe. For example, you might say that a student is so motivated to get into a clinical psychology program that she spends every night studying. An athlete is so motivated to become a starting quarterback that he spends every spare moment watching film and polishing his throwing and running and ball handling skills.

Anyone who has ever set a goal (lose 22 pounds or run a marathon) probably immediately realizes that simply having the desire to accomplish something is not enough. Achieving such a goal requires the ability to persist through obstacles and endurance to keep going in spite of difficulties.

COMPONENTS OF MOTIVATION

What exactly lies behind the motivations for why we act? Psychologists have proposed different theories of motivation, including drive theory, instinct theory, and humanistic theory. The reality is that there are many different forces that guide and direct our motivations, all of which can be divided into three major components: activation, persistence, and intensity.

Activation involves the decision to initiate a behavior, such as enrolling in a psychology class and get to team practice early and stay late to work on improving your personal skills.

Persistence is the continued effort toward a goal even though obstacles may exist. An example of persistence would be taking more psychology courses in order to earn a degree although it requires a significant investment of time, energy, and resources. Doing more 'reps' than any other teammate who plays your position to make sure you are the very best version of yourself.

Intensity can be seen in the concentration and vigor that goes into pursuing a goal. For example, one student might coast by without much effort, while another student will study regularly, participate in discussions, and take advantage of research opportunities outside of class. The first student lacks intensity, while the second pursues his educational goals with greater intensity.

THEORIES OF MOTIVATION
(Intrinsic Verses Extrinsic)

What are the things that actually motivate us to act? Psychologists have categorized them into either Extrinsic or Intrinsic motivation. Extrinsic motivations are those that arise from outside of the individual and often involve rewards such as trophies, money, social recognition, or praise. Intrinsic motivations are those that arise from within the individual, such as doing a complicated crossword puzzle purely for the personal gratification of solving a problem.

Within these two categories of Intrinsic and Extrinsic, psychologists have proposed three different theories to explain motivation:

Instincts: The instinct theory of motivation suggests that behaviors are motivated by instincts, which are fixed and inborn patterns of behavior. Psychologists including W. James, Freud, Maslow and McDougal have proposed a number of basic human drives that motivate behavior. Such instincts might include biological instincts that are important for an organism's survival such as fear, cleanliness, and love.

Drives and Needs: Many of your behaviors such as eating, drinking, and sleeping are motivated by a biological need for food, water, and rest. Therefore, you are motivated to eat, drink, and sleep. Drive theory suggests that people have basic biological drives and that your behaviors are motivated by the need to fulfill these drives.

Arousal Levels: The arousal theory of motivation suggests that people are motivated to engage in behaviors that help them maintain their optimal level of arousal. A person with low arousal needs might pursue relaxing activities such as reading a book, while those with high arousal needs might be motivated to engage in exciting, thrill-seeking behaviors, such as motorcycle racing.

ROOT CAUSES OF LACK OF MOTIVATION

Motivation is a process that controls and maintains certain behaviors. Eating chocolate, exercising, studying, and avoiding triggers to prevent an alcoholic relapse all require motivation. Everyone experiences lack of motivation from time to time. Staring at a stack of books not wanting to study, seeing a pile of dishes in the sink and not feeling like doing them or skipping going to the gym because you don't feel like it are all signs of lack of motivation.

For some people, trouble feeling motivated can have negative impact on academic, personal or professional success. Low grades, damaged friendships or a demotion at work are all realistic consequences of low motivation. Addressing the root cause of motivation issues is the first step in learning how to reengage in healthy behaviors.

The seven most common reasons why people have trouble motivating themselves include:

Depression

One of the most common symptoms of depression is called Anhedonia, which is a diverse array of deficits in motivation and ability to experience pleasure – including reduced anticipatory pleasure (wanting), reduced consummator pleasure (liking), and deficits in reinforcement learning or the lack of interest in activities. Depression can wreak havoc on academic and professional success. Treating the depression generally has a very positive effect on motivation and productivity. That is, when it is the correct diagnosis and the correct treatment required to deal with each individual person and his/her situation.

When I was paralyzed playing football and I hit rock bottom and thought I was depressed, in reality I was not depressed. Some people we know, who could include you, family members, friends, coworkers and teammates, have been clinically diagnosed by a responsible physician as having a chemical imbalance. With this professional assessment comes a required prescribed medication that is part of the therapeutic solution. And when we know someone who is facing this challenge we need to give them nonjudgmental friendship, respect, support and unconditional love!

However, when I was injured at football practice I didn't suddenly get a 'chemical imbalance' where I needed medication to recover. There is a giant difference between being depressed and disappointed – a giant difference between being depressed and discouraged – a giant difference between being depressed and having my heart broken and my dreams shattered, which can only be remedied by dreaming a new dream and moving forward with the understanding that "Pain is a signal to grow, not to suffer. Once we learn the lesson the pain is teaching us, the pain goes away." Nothing happens 'to' us, only 'for us, to make us stronger, give us experience and remind us that in life there are no mistakes, only lessons. We never lose if we always learn!

Most so-called depression can be overcome when we remember the acronym H.A.L.T.S., which reminds us to avoid being Hungry, Angry, Lonely, Tired and Sad. Whenever we experience any one or more of these emotionally distorting physical and attitudinal predicaments we cannot deeply feel and communicate on a high level of compassion, understanding and connection. Research shows that the two major reasons people attempt suicide is a feeling of hopelessness and a lack of human connection. Medicating someone who is not chemically unbalanced is malpractice and a gross misdiagnosis by an irresponsible doctor who should be punished to the full extent of the law for trying to mitigate a suffering soul by flat lining his/her human spirit and inherent instinct to fight or flee (Not Give Up).

What most of us need to remedy a so-called depressive attitude is to simply remember, revisit and reactivate the emotionally stimulating motivational power that comes from within when we dream a mighty dream that inspires us to redefine what's possible and turn it into a goal that requires action and "satisfaction to completion."

Fear of Failure

Many parents with perfectionistic attitudes teach their children that mistakes are failures and that they are flawed people. This develops an inherent fear of failure, which is presented by avoiding work. Instead, people who are afraid of failing avoid setting a goal because it feels safer than trying and not succeeding.

Low Self-Esteem

People who have low self-esteem tend to believe that they are not capable of succeeding and often self-sabotage. They will miss deadlines, procrastinate, double-book or put in minimal effort so that when the project or task is not perfectly complete, there is something else to blame. Deflecting personal responsibility helps preserve a delicate sense of self that comes with low self-esteem.

Blaming / Complaining

Although you are a leader, manager, mentor or coach, imagine yourself as a therapist, and a young woman comes into your office and starts to yell and cry and whine that the reason her life is out of control is because of her father; that her dear old dad is the cause of her pain and misery. What council would you give her? Would you suggest bringing in her father so you could begin treating him? It is only logical that if he is the cause of her woes, if you cure him, her pain should go away?

Because of scenarios like this, Blaming and Complaining rank at the top of the causes for losing our motivation. The only way out of this attitudinal rut is to start taking full responsibility for your every thought and action. When you stop and refine your thinking to take 100% responsibility, you realize that you're either participating in creating that situation or allowing it to continue.

This also applies Complaining. In order to complain, you've got to have a reference point of something you want; an item or a situation that is better than what you have now or more desirable than what someone else has something you have not been willing to risk creating. So you feel entitled to complain about it instead.

When someone is complaining about something it means they know there is something they can do about it, because people don't usually complain about the things they cannot change. The ironic truth is that complainers usually whine and voice their complaints to those who can't do anything about the issues.

Lack of Interest

Some tasks are uninteresting and that makes them difficult to engage in. People require frequent rewards and if the school subject or project is not interesting enough, it is natural to not participate in it. This becomes especially problematic when students are involved in a major, class or career that is uninteresting. Their attention will be diverted elsewhere, resulting in poor grades or low performance at work.

Procrastination

Procrastination occurs for a variety of reasons, including feeling overwhelmed, being depressed, feeling anxious or fearing failure among others. When procrastination becomes a habit, it may appear that the person is not motivated in succeeding.

Stress / Overwhelm

Stress takes up a significant amount of cognitive and emotional bandwidth. Some people cope with stress and feeling overwhelmed by avoiding deadlines or finding triggers to engage in substance use again. Lack of sleep due to stress or overwhelm can also make it difficult to feel motivated.

REFOCUSING ON 'WHY' / REIGNITING MOTIVATION

When someone claims he is "burned out" that is good news because it means that once upon a time he was "lit!" And it takes a lot less effort to reignite and re-light a flicker and turn it into a flame that once burned brightly! Which means the solution remedies to getting motivated again are simple and divided into two areas: mental perception and physical reality.

Attitudinal Solutions

- Today you have never been this old before, and today you will never be this young again. So right now and every right now matters.
- What happens to you is not nearly as important as how you respond.
- When you are Hungry, Angry, Lonely, Tired, or Sad replace hunger with nutritious food; anger with forgiveness; loneliness with service; tiredness (which makes cowards of us all) with exercise and rest; and sadness with a personal dream.
- Motivation is adding value to value. We don't have to see the whole staircase to take the first step. We need only see and feel the value of taking the next step, realizing that courage is staying one step ahead of fear.

Behavioral Solutions

- Exercise, taking a break from the task at hand as well as maintaining healthy eating and sleeping patterns all help in improving your mood, anxiety and stress.
- It's easier to act your way into positive thinking than to think your way into positive action. It's not the sugar that makes the tea sweet it's the stirring.

- Regardless if we are leisurely strolling in the park, competing in the Olympic Games, climbing Mount Everest, or striving to be significant, one step at a time is good walking, one step at a time is good running, one step at a time is good climbing, and one day at a time is good living! To finish first, you must first finish!

You are never too young or too old to uncover your talents, go after what you want and achieve extraordinary success:

- Helen Keller, at the age of 19 months, became deaf and blind. But that didn't stop her. She was the first deaf and blind person to earn a Bachelor of Arts degree.
- Mozart was already competent on keyboard and violin; he composed from the age of 5.
- Shirley Temple was 6 when she became a movie star on "Bright Eyes."
- Anne Frank was 12 when she wrote the diary of Anne Frank.
- Magnus Carlsen became a chess Grandmaster at the age of 13.
- Nadia Comăneci was a gymnast from Romania who scored seven perfect 10.0 and won three gold medals at the Olympics at age 14.
- Tenzin Gyatso was formally recognized as the 14th Dalai Lama in November 1950, at the age of 15.
- Pele, a soccer superstar, was 17 years old when he won the world cup in 1958 with Brazil.
- Elvis was a superstar by age 19.

- John Lennon was 20 years old and Paul McCartney was 18 when the Beatles had their first concert in 1961.
- Jesse Owens was 22 when he won 4 Olympic gold medals in Berlin 1936.
- Beethoven was a piano virtuoso by age 23
- Isaac Newton wrote Philosophiæ Naturalis Principia Mathematica at age 24
- Roger Bannister was 25 when he broke the 4-minute mile record
- Albert Einstein was 26 when he wrote the theory of relativity
- Michelangelo created two of the greatest sculptures "David" and "Pieta" by age 28
- Alexander the Great, by age 29, had created one of the largest empires of the ancient world
- J.K. Rowling was 30 years old when she finished the first manuscript of Harry Potter
- Amelia Earhart was 31 years old when she became the first woman to fly solo across the Atlantic Ocean
- Oprah was 32 when she started her talk show, which has become the highest-rated program of its kind
- Sir Edmund Hillary was 33 when he became the first man to summit Mount Everest
- Martin Luther King Jr. was 34 when he delivered his speech "I Have a Dream."
- Marie Curie was 35 years old when she was nominated for a Nobel Prize in Physics
- The Wright brothers, Orville (32) and Wilbur (36) invented and built the world's first successful

airplane and making the first controlled, powered and sustained heavier-than-air human flight

- Vincent Van Gogh was 37 when he died virtually unknown, yet his paintings today are worth millions.
- Neil Armstrong was 38 when he became the first man to set foot on the moon.
- Mark Twain was 40 when he wrote "The Adventures of Tom Sawyer", and 49 years old when he wrote "Adventures of Huckleberry Finn"
- Christopher Columbus was 41 when he discovered the Americas
- Rosa Parks was 42 when she refused to obey the bus driver's order to give up her seat to make room for a white passenger
- John F. Kennedy was 43 years old when he became President of the United States
- Henry Ford was 45 when the Model T came out.
- Suzanne Collins was 46 when she wrote "The Hunger Games"
- Charles Darwin was 50 years old when his book On the Origin of Species came out.
- Leonardo Da Vinci was 51 years old when he painted the Mona Lisa.
- Abraham Lincoln was 52 when he became president.
- Ray Kroc Was 53 when he bought the McDonalds Franchise and took it to unprecedented levels.
- Dr. Seuss was 54 when he wrote "The Cat in the Hat".
- Colonel Harland Sanders was 61 when he started the KFC Franchise

- J.R.R Tolkien was 62 when the Lord of the Ring books came out
- Ronald Reagan was 69 when he became President of the US
- Nelson Mandela was 76 when he became President of the new South Africa

CHAPTER FIVE

THINKING BIG / TAKING CHARGE

We all have "bucket lists" that consist of exciting adventures we dream about achieving and accomplishing before we die. Because of my thirty-year involvement with the US military, my list has included flying every plane and helicopter in the US Air Force, Navy, Marines, and Army inventory. Depending on the aircraft, the sorties usually last for at least ninety minutes, wherein I have had the opportunity to fly them for thirty minutes.

So far I have flown the Black Hawk and Apache helicopters; the T-38, F-4, F-15, F- 16, and F-18 fighter jets; the C- 130, C-5, and C-17 transporters; the KC-10 and KC-135 tankers; the B-1, B-2, and B-52 bombers; and the U-2 spy plane, where for approximately three hours – at more than 70,000 feet – I saw the curvature of the earth, looked into the blackness of space, and pondered eternity and my place in it.

Anybody can learn to fly an airplane, but it takes a special individual to be a high-performance pilot. I have experienced every time I have interacted with the US military. General Patton put it in perspective when he explained, "Wars may be fought with weapons, but they are won by men. It is the spirit of the men who follow and of the man who leads that gains the victory. If you are going to win any battle, you have to make the mind run the body. Never let the body tell the mind what to do."

I was an eyewitness to this at the end of 2000. I was invited to speak at the US Navy Commanders Conference at the Naval Museum in Pensacola, Florida. It was a wonderful experience, and I felt a deep connection with the audience of military brass. After my speech, the admirals congratulated me and said to let them know if there was anything they could ever do for me. I didn't even have to think about it. I quickly replied that I'd always dreamed of a backseat ride in an F-18 fighter jet. Without even blinking, US Marine pilot Colonel Eugene Frazier (call sign "Gator") said, "It's done. We can do that! Your training will be tough. We will cut you no slack. You're going to have to want it bad! Most VIPs have not made it through and did not get to fly. It's a gut check that is mind over matter — will over skill!"

TOP GUN TRAINING

On January 16, 2001, I went through five long, grueling hours of intense safety and survival training at the Naval Test

Pilot School at Patuxent River, Maryland, in preparation for my flight the following morning. My first requirement was a complete physical examination by the flight surgeon.

Then it was off to "Aviation Physiology Water Survival Training." In eighty pounds of full combat gear, I had to swim fifty yards, two full lengths of an Olympic- size swimming pool (down and back), and then tread water for fifteen minutes. After a short rest out of the pool, with a blindfold mask covering my helmet, I then had to jump back in to find my way out of an underwater maze to simulate being trapped in the cockpit and keeping my wits about me to survive.

Next, I sat through a lecture with diagrams and a test on "spatial disorientation." They strapped me into a souped-up bar stool with a seat belt, spun me around for five minutes, and had me get off and find my way to the door. (I felt like I was at a fraternity party in college!)

Next was "Egress Training," where I met a Rambo -looking guy, who, with a Southern accent, huge muscles, and a "yee haw" look in his eye, asked, "Ya ever eject out of a jet before?" I sheepishly grunted the Scooby Doo "Hurh?" As he walked closer, I read his name-tag call sign: "Psycho." He immediately strapped me onto a tall torture-chamber-looking sled that rose to the ceiling at a forty-five -degree angle about fifty-five feet high. He smiled. "Keep your head up and back, knees straight, and elbows in, and on three, pull the yellow handle between your legs."

"What?"

"Three!"

I pulled and with three Gs of force squishing my body against itself, I shot up to the end of this ejection seat practice sled. We did it three times. Rambo then instructed me in the graceful art of flying and steering my parachute by hanging me from a ten -foot bar with straps that pinched me to where I didn't know if he had castrated me or was giving me a ninety-mile-an-hour enema! I was finally cut loose, concluding our wonderful time together by roll landing off a five-foot wall to simulate the hard landing.

Next on the training schedule was "Altitude Acclamation," where they took me to a room, fitted me with an oxygen mask, and simulated being at high altitude and losing air. I played a game of simply putting pegs into the correct round or square hole and thought I was doing it correctly. Come to find out on the video replay, I wasn't, and they documented at what level and point I began to lose my full faculties. They instructed me on what to do in case this lack of oxygen episode did occur. At day's end, I was required to take a classroom written exam on the contents and operation of every item in my survival vest, followed by a description of the cockpit gauges and "heads-up display," and how to hook up and release all the oxygen hoses, communication lines, safety belts, bells, and whistles.

Why do I itemize with such detail? Because I almost flunked the test! I nearly drowned three times! I was dizzy and exhausted, yet I continued on. Why? Of course it was to find Kelly McGillis in a washroom and get her to fall in love with me while I was flying Mach 2 with my hair on fire!

That night, I had a full five-course dinner with my host, Colonel Frazier, at the Officers Club. I asked him if there was anything special I should eat for breakfast, and he said, "Bananas."

"Why?" I asked. "Potassium? Will I cramp up?"

He said, "No, it's because bananas taste exactly the same going in as they do coming out."

TOP GUN FLYING

The next day, January 17, I flew with Commander Reuter – call sign "Roto" – on a ride to remember. There was no Cougar or Maverick or Iceman. I was putting my life in the hands of Roto Reuter! Turns out he was awesome and had more aircraft carrier takeoffs and landings than anyone else on base. The coolest thing was that he was a legitimate "Top Gunner" – one of the best of the best naval aviators.

He even walked and smiled like Tom Cruise! Before we left the locker room to walk out on the tarmac, he taught me how to be cool by holding my helmet like a football in the crook of my elbow and how to walk and then stand like a real fighter pilot by the plane when we finally met the photographers for the "hero shots."

We took off in a straight- up, full, after-burner climb, and for the next ninety minutes, we did every Top Gun movie maneuver and more – loops, barrel rolls, yanks, and banks. We dived, climbed, and dived again with a vertical velocity of

10,000 feet per minute. We did ninety-degree turns at 600 mph, and for one special maneuver, climbed even higher to shoot straight down to pick up more speed (as if we weren't going fast enough as it was!). With my face now crammed up against the cockpit window, we climbed straight up to more than 55,000 feet, where you could actually begin to see the black sky and the curvature of the earth.

Then we went upside down, flipped over to inside out, and flew in formation with a second aircraft we rendezvoused with. We executed attack bombing runs on a makeshift ship at the practice range in North Carolina, flew at 640 knots at only 500 feet off the ground, then went back to the thin air at 46,000 feet altitude where we broke the sound barrier going Mach 1.9 (around 1,200 mph – twice the speed of sound) . We caught seven Gs in some of our turns (which is seven times my 235-pound body weight being smashed against my face, back, chest, kneecaps, and toes). I felt like somebody grabbed my bottom lip and pulled it up over my head.

All this took place in a ninety- minute rock-and-roller-coaster ride every mentally irregular lunatic yearns for at Seven Flags over Hell Psycho Park. The highlight was my opportunity to fly the F-18 for thirty of the ninety minutes.

Before I share what I learned, let me confess to what everyone wonders. Colonel Frasier was absolutely right about the bananas, and yes, I egressed (ejected) all five dinner courses from the previous evening and even ejected some Hot Tamales I had eaten at a movie when I was nine! We were upside down so long that I am probably the only guy alive who has ever "thrown down!" Ha!

TOP GUN LESSON

When we landed and I put my face back in the middle of my head, I asked Roto to point out some details about the plane. Commander Reuter explained that the F-18 Hornet is a state-of -the-art, high-tech, finely tuned and designed machine that costs $50 million to build.

'Hoss," he said (it was now my 'call sign' – no one ever gets to choose their own call sign and I barely fit in the seat), "the cockpit is crammed full of high-tech gauges, gadgets, switches, and screens. As you noticed, the control stick came out of the floor and was straddled between our knees. The stick only moved three inches forward, three inches left and right, and five inches backward. We needed to move the control stick only one inch in either one of those four directions, and it immediately changed the direction of the aircraft forty-five degrees."

So I asked him how we flew this magnificent flying machine. Flippantly he said, "By feel."

Startled by his answer I asked, "What do you mean?"

With a smile he answered, "We became the plane. We remained analog in a digital environment – and controlled high tech with high touch!"

Wow! We know the brain has two sides: the left cognitive/logical side and the right emotional/creative side. I find it interesting that we fly a supersonic, high performance fighter jet with the touchy-feely, passionate, imaginative, and intuitive right side of the brain.

F-16 FINALE

Shortly after this experience, I was given my first ride in an Air Force F-16 Falcon, wherein we caught 9.4 Gs and went Mach 1.1 while engaging in an air-to-air combat exercise where we chased another F-16 and then it chased us. Upon landing, I asked my pilot, Colonel Bill "Coutter" Couts, to explain how we flew this incredible F-16 with its patented "fly -by -wire" control grip that only moved one-eighth to three eighths of an inch in any direction.

He answered, "Hot Lips" (yes, that is my Air Force call sign!), "when you climbed up the ladder and slid into the cockpit, did you strap into the F-16, or did you strap the F-16 on to you?"

To me, and for those whom I am responsible to teach and mold and build into a winning team, this message is Motivation

101, Inspiration 202, Advanced Leadership 303, and the Art of Significance – Achieving the Level beyond Success!

Bottom line: The only thing we are not in charge of is whether or not we are in charge. High-performance leadership, management, selling, teaching, parenting, coaching and living is about Thinking Big, Figuring It Out, Feeling It, Taking Charge, strapping it on and going Mach II with your hair on fire! Only when you do, are you qualified and respected enough to inspire and expect others to do the same!

CHAPTER SIX

IMPLEMENTING EXPECTATIONS

*"There is a difference between
training to fight and training to win."*

Cassius Marcellus Clay Jr., as Muhammad Ali was once known, was born in Louisville, Kentucky, on January 17, 1942. During Ali's youth, Louisville was a city of segregated public facilities, the Kentucky Derby, and other symbols of the Southern white aristocracy. African Americans were the servants and poor working class. The grandest dreams available to them were being a preacher or a teacher in an all-black church or school.

Young Cassius was intense and full of dreams, which in this environment brought frustration. He knew he was somebody and needed to somehow vent his societal suppression. That's when he discovered boxing. At twelve years of age and eighty-nine pounds, young Cassius had his first official boxing match. He won by a split decision and immediately started jumping up and down yelling, "I am the greatest. I will be the greatest fighter who ever lived."

Years later, a childhood classmate remembered, "We were in elementary school together and Cassius was just another one of the kids. You push and you shove each other, and get into the normal fights. There were days he lost and days he won. So when he beat Sonny Liston to win the heavyweight championship, we all started laughing, saying, 'He's not even undefeated in the neighborhood. How can he be champion of the world?'"

I can't exactly explain why, but probably the most prestigious award, accomplishment, or title in all of sports is to win the heavyweight boxing championship of the world. Cassius Clay won the championship, converted to the Muslim faith, changed his name to Muhammad Ali, was stripped of his title for refusing induction into the US Army on religious grounds, and won the championship back two more times. He truly is the greatest. He is not only the most famous fighter who ever lived, but the most famous athlete and most recognized face in the world.

As a teenager, I had been a Golden Gloves boxer, and Ali had been my idol. I emulated everything he did from tassels on my boots to the Ali Shuffle, rope-a-dope, and taunting jab. With fast hands and a desire to beat everybody, I was known as the "Great White Hope." Each time I fought, instead of chanting, "Danny, Danny," my friends chanted, "Dali, Dali!" Muhammad Ali truly was my hero, and I would have given anything to meet him.

Years later, in 1988, I had just finished speaking to the students of Andrews University in Berrien Springs, Michigan. I was in the Union Building signing books when I overheard some students talking about seeing Muhammad Ali on campus. I was so excited I could hardly ask where. They informed me that he was gone, but it was no big deal because he lived there and visited the school often. I immediately excused myself and asked the two gentlemen who were driving me around to grab a camera and take me to Ali's home. They told me I was fooling myself if I thought I could meet him. They stopped at the big white wall and giant iron-gate at the edge of a long, curving driveway. I got out and walked the hundred yards to his beautiful home. His eighty-eight acres had previously belonged to the Chicago gangster Al Capone, and "Muhammad Ali Farms," as Ali called it, was an amazing sight.

'F.E.A.R. MEANS FALSE EVIDENCE APPEARING REAL'

With my heart pounding, I took a deep breath to calm my fear, and knocked on the front door. A beautiful woman answered. I knew from photographs that she was his lovely wife. She asked, "May I help you?" I said, "Yes ma'am. Is Muhammad in?" She asked, "May I tell him who is calling?" Sheepishly, I replied, "Sure, Dan Clark." She walked away, and within seconds, an imposing six-foot-three-inch, 225- pound world champion, world peace ambassador, advocate of human rights, living legend, and idol filled the entire doorway.

Muhammad simply smiled his famous smile and in his quiet, breathy voice invited me in. I excused myself for a minute, sprinted to the garden to where my friends could see me and wildly waved my arms and whistled for them to come in.

In 1988, Muhammad's Parkinson's disease had not yet taken away his speech. Although he was a little slow, he talked up a storm. The next four and a half hours, we sat in his living room and watched his greatest fights: the 'Thrilla in Manila,' the 'Rumble in the Jungle,' and more. With his own personal commentary, jokes, and stories, he made every move come alive. Later he even performed some of his favorite magic tricks.

As this mind-boggling experience started coming to an end he asked me if I had any questions. After a moment I asked, "You are a three-time champion, which means you were twice defeated by inferior opponents. Leon Spinks? Seriously?" Ali smiled. "What happened?"

Without missing a beat Ali explained, "I got complacent and took my opportunities for granted, and tried to live off my past laurels and successes. Have you ever done that?"

Obviously I agreed and asked what he learned that allowed him to win the championship the third time. His answer not only intensified my sense of urgency and elevated my understanding of the significance of work ethic, but because of what he said, I have committed to being 'brilliant at the basics' in everything I do. Ali said, "Every time I climbed into the ring I realized I no longer held the title. I had put it up for grabs and must fight s hard as I did the first time I won it, to win it back!"

As we were saying our goodbyes and promising to keep in touch, the most incredible thing happened that changed my life forever. Ali asked me, "Did you ever fight?" I nodded yes, and he said, "Let me see your left hook." We both put our hands up and started to playfully spar and dance around. I broke into the Ali Shuffle, and he kidded me, "That's not the Shuffle, that's the Clark Scuffle!"

He then got right in my face and said, "Everybody knows I'm the greatest, but so are you. Repeat with me, 'I am the greatest.'" I repeated it and he said, "Louder, with more heart." I repeated it, and he said, "No, like your man Rocky. Mean it, man, mean it. Say it like you want to beat Joe Frazier. Say it like you want to punch George Foreman. Say it to me like I'm Howard Cosell!" One more time he yelled, "I am the greatest," and again had me mimic him. He then put his arm around me, gave me a big hug, looked me square in the eyes, and whispered in his breathy voice, "How do you feel? Do you believe it? I do."

It's been many years since that wonderful day, but I remember it every time I walk past the photos of us hung on my basement "Wall of Fame." Whenever I am discouraged and feel that I can't go on anymore, I relive Ali looking me square in the eyes and convincing me that, "I am the greatest." I guarantee he is, and he wants each of us to believe that we can be, too.

After a 32-year battle with Parkinson's disease, Muhammad Ali passed away on June 3, 2016, at the age of 74. The three -time World Heavyweight Champion had suffered for three decades from Parkinson's, a progressive neurological condition that slowly robbed him of both his verbal grace and his physical dexterity. Until we meet again, may you rest in peace.

CHAPTER SEVEN

TRIBUTE TO PREPARATION

"Don't wish it was easier; wish you were better. If you are not willing to risk the unusual, you will have to settle for the ordinary. The few who do are the envy of the many who only watch." —Jim Rohn

Wayne Gretzky is clearly the greatest hockey player to ever play the game. He has influenced the lives of many young players. Wayne says that the greatest single influence in his life is his father, Walter. Walt was his coach, his mentor, and has always been and will always be his best friend. Wayne's greatest honor comes when he is introduced as Walter Gretzky's son.

I had the honor of talking with Wayne, but the greatest thrill was spending two days with Walter in his home in Brantford, Ontario, Canada. We played golf; laughed; toured his famous basement full of Wayne's MVP awards, trophies, autographed sticks, skates, and jerseys; laughed some more; and swapped countless inspirational stories. Walt is extremely smart and very intense, yet warm and engaging. He is a deeply committed family man and is community -oriented in his tireless efforts to help charitable organizations. Even today, he coaches junior hockey teams and touches hundreds of young people's lives each year. With Walt as his dad, it is obvious why Wayne is such a clean, powerful, positive role model and an elegant gentleman.

Walt is famous for saying, "You miss 100 percent of the shots you don't take." Wayne is famous for answering the question, "Why are you the greatest player?" with the highly quoted response, "Most players go to where the puck is. I go to where the puck is going to be." Yes, Wayne Gretzky teaches us about anticipation, but according to his dad, Wayne teaches us even more about preparation.

If you want to discover why Wayne is the greatest hockey player who ever lived, don't watch him on the ice – watch him when he is on the bench. He studies every player to see where they go, how they pass, to whom they pass, which side they favor, how they fight, if they can defend going backward, and who they favor in certain playmaking situations. By the time Wayne hits the ice, he knows exactly where to go to intercept a pass, where to block a shot, and when to skate into the spacing lanes of the other team to get the competitive advantage to shoot and score. Preparation is why Wayne Gretzky is hockey's all-time leading scorer.

Walt told me Wayne was also an exceptional baseball player. Wayne was named to the all-star team every year since he was nine years old. He was an extraordinary pitcher. Wayne wanted to practice every day, but most of his friends were out doing the playful things little guys like to do – riding bikes, hiking, catching lizards. So Wayne would bribe his friends by paying them a quarter to play goalie while he took 100 shots and another quarter to catch while he threw 100 pitches.

These kids would oftentimes go home with sore hands, black eyes, and bloody noses from their inability to stop his extremely hard, fast shots and pitches. By the time Wayne was a teenager he had a ninety-mile-an-hour fastball. Walt told me it was amazing to watch Wayne pitch. Even if the batters hit against him in the first couple of innings, by the time Wayne had faced each of them once, he remembered their strengths and weaknesses and struck them out from then on.

Walt told me Wayne is a perfectionist and used to practice the same shot from the same place on the ice hundreds of times in an afternoon. When most kids lost interest and concentration, Wayne would somehow kick it into a higher gear and endure until he succeeded at what he was trying to accomplish. He even practiced hitting the puck off certain places in the hockey rink baseboards so he would know exactly where the puck was going to be when it ricocheted. Wayne's desire to prepare was so intense that he convinced his dad to build a hockey rink in the backyard and flood it in the winter, which allowed Wayne to start practicing at the crack of dawn and continue until the neighbors complained late at night about the noise. The only thing that took Wayne off the ice was his dad's reminder that he needed to go to bed and rest so he could wake up refreshed, alert, and ready to do it again the next day.

Having met Wayne, I can say that his preparation philosophy of "leaving no regrets" paid its greatest dividend when his dear, sweet dad had a brain aneurysm at the age of fifty-four. When Wayne received the late-night emergency phone call in Los Angeles, he rushed to be at his dying father's bedside. When he arrived, the doctors told Wayne there was very little hope.

Wayne ignored the prognosis and sat for hours and hours talking to his dad and stroking his arm. He found strength in the knowledge that he had no regrets. He had said all the things he needed to say to his hero many times before this tragedy occurred. He had already spent more time with his dad than most children spend with their dads in an entire lifetime. Clearly, Wayne was prepared for the worst, which allowed him to be strong for others and focus his energy on praying, hoping, and coaxing his dad to hang tough and pull through. Even more important than Wayne's preparation, however, was the fact that the nurses were prepared, and the hospital staff was prepared, and a specialist doctor – who was one of the only physicians in the world prepared to perform the intricate surgery – was willing to come out of retirement because he was prepared.

Walter Gretzky miraculously recovered and remains the number one influence in Wayne's life today. And the message? Preparation not only gave Wayne his life, it also saved Walter from death. Gretzky is not the greatest hockey player who ever lived simply because he can anticipate. Wayne is the Great One because his dad taught him to relentlessly pursue perfection through preparation.

ULTIMATE PREPARATION IS ANSWERING WHAT, WHY, HOW AND WHEN

It was the last football game of Brian's senior year, and a message came that his father had died. When the coach found out, he decided to tell Brian before the game, knowing he probably would elect not to play. But instead of reacting sorrowfully, Brian just took it all in stride and said, "I'll leave right after the game."

The coach had heard Brian speak highly of his father and expected him to grieve. When he didn't, the coach said, "Brian, you don't have to play. This game isn't that important."

Brian ignored him and played the game anyway. And play he did. Brian was the star, winning the game as a man possessed. In the locker room, the other players showered with Brian. Some offered condolences, but most were appalled at his lack of sorrow. Brian was casual and happy, as if nothing had gone wrong. The coach was angry and worried that he had taught too much devotion to sports and not enough compassion. He scolded Brian, "Why did you play the game? Your father is dead. I'm ashamed of you and of myself."

Brian replied, "Coach, this was our last game. I am a senior. I had to play. This was the first time my dad has ever seen me play, and I had to play like I never played before." The coach didn't understand.

With tears streaming down his cheeks, Brian replied, "You didn't know my father was blind, did you?"

CHAPTER EIGHT

JOINT/SHARED EXPECTATIONS

"The only place from which a person can grow is where he/she is. We must go where they are physical and emotionally. Only there can we gently invite him/her to improve." —Dan Clark

Setting Joint Expectations is Cooperative Collaboration. A good example of how internal and external expectations interface and impact a team's performance and productivity is found within every team in the National Football League. I divide them into four groups:

The internal expectation of the head coach is to win because his contract and job security are based 100 percent on winning. His external expectation from the owner is to also win. If he loses he gets fired. In the nine years Brian Billick was the head coach of the Baltimore Ravens, during which time he won Super Bowl XXXV, there were over 100 coaches fired or rotated to other teams because they could not consistently win. The Washington Redskins had five different head coaches in the same nine years! Ironically, one of the primary reasons a corporation fails is because of a constant turn over in CEOs and high-level leadership.

The second group consists of the majority of the players who have been in the league for over five years and have an internal expectation to just stay relevant and do their jobs. Until something drastically changes that shows them they have a chance to win (the hiring of a new winning coach – better players acquired) the external expectations can change, but these players won't.

The third group is the new rookies coming into the league who might say publically that they want to win, but for them it's only about internal expectations – it's only about the "contract."

The first NFL contract is a four-year deal. Unless they are drafted in the first round with guaranteed money, each rookie must still get through training camp and the pre-season and make the final 53- player roster. Most teams invite 100 players to training camp and cut it down to 53 by the final pre-season game.

From this first internal expectation comes the rookie's next one focused on playing time, rushing yards, tackles made, and passes thrown, caught, or intercepted.

Based on his performance, a rookie's third internal expectation is to sign his second four-year contract, which is now much bigger and filled with bonuses because of his personal performance in his first contract.

Only when the rookie has signed this "security deal" and taken care of Maslow's need of personal/physical comfort, does he emotionally and physically buy into the external expectations of his team and winning the Super Bowl.

The final group on the team is the three to four superstar veteran players who are on their second or third contract, who have already compiled their amazing personal stats, and now have the singular internal expectation to win the Super Bowl.

The external expectation from the owners and coaches is to also win the Super Bowl – that's why they are being paid the big bucks.

Statistically, most teams will win and lose 30 percent of their games every season. The outcome of the remaining 40 percent of their games will be determined by external expectations, how many of the players fully buy into them, and make them their own.

WE MUST WIN ON AND OFF THE SCOREBOARD

Only when high internal expectations match high external expectations can we reach peak performance and achieve our desired results of Building A Winning Team, Dominating Our Competition, Creating An Organizational Dynasty, and transforming our organizations from Successful to Significant.

A friend of mine experienced a miracle in a Mesa, Arizona, school that caters to learning disabled children. Randy Gray's young boy diligently does everything he can to learn and grow in strength. Every day, Randy stops by the school after work so the two of them can walk home together.

One afternoon, they walked past a park where some young men the boy knew were playing baseball. The boy asked, "Do you think they will let me play?" His father knew that his son was not athletic, and because of his disabilities, most boys would not want him on their team. But his father understood that if his son was allowed to play, it would give him a much-needed sense of belonging.

The boy's father approached one of the young men and asked if his son could play. The boy looked around for guidance from his teammates. Getting none, he took matters into his own hands and said, "We're losing by six runs, and the game is in the eighth inning. I guess he can be on our team and we'll try to put him up to bat in the ninth inning." The father was ecstatic as his son smiled broadly.

In the bottom on the eighth inning, the losing team scored a few runs but was still behind by three. In the bottom of the ninth, the boy's team scored again, and now with two outs and the bases loaded, with the potential winning run on base, Randy's son was scheduled to be up to bat. Would the team actually let him bat at this juncture and give away their chance to win the game?

Surprisingly, the boy was given the bat. Everyone knew he was mentally and physically challenged. The boy didn't even know how to hold the bat properly, let alone hit. However, as he stepped up to the plate, the pitcher moved up a few steps to lob the ball in softly so he could at least make contact. The first pitch came in and the boy swung clumsily and missed. One of his teammates ran to him, and together they held the bat and faced the pitcher, waiting for the next throw. The pitcher again took a few steps forward to toss the ball softly toward the determined little boy. As the pitch came in, he and his teammate swung the bat, and together they hit a slow ground ball to the pitcher.

The pitcher picked up the soft grounder and could easily have thrown the ball to the first baseman. The little boy would have been out by a mile, and that would have ended the game. Instead, the pitcher took the ball and threw it on a high arc to right field, far beyond reach of the first baseman. Everyone started yelling, "Run, buddy, run to first. Run to first!" Never in his life had the boy run to first.

He scampered and limped down the baseline wide-eyed and startled. By the time he reached first base, the right fielder had the ball. He could have thrown the ball to the second baseman who would have tagged him out, but the right fielder understood what the pitcher's intentions were, so he threw the ball high and far over the third baseman's head. Everyone yelled, "Run to second, run to second." Again, startled, but with a grin on his face so big he could have eaten a banana sideways, the little guy ran.

As he reached second base, the opposing shortstop ran to him, turned him in the direction of third base, and shouted, "Run to third." As he rounded third, the nine boys from each team ran behind him screaming, "Run, little buddy, run home!" He ran home and stepped on home plate. All eighteen boys from both teams lifted him on their shoulders and made him the hero. He had just hit a "grand slam" and won the game for his team!

With tears rolling down his face, Randy softly whispered, "I witnessed a real miracle that day. Not only did those eighteen boys realize the power of empathy, compassion, and service above self, but they let a father and his struggling son share together the power of a dream and the power of emotional connection that comes only through the magic of unconditional love!"

ATTITUDE IS EVERYTHING

When my son, Spencer, was in the first grade, he was having trouble saying his Rs. We thought it was cute until one day Spencer came home with tears in his eyes. I asked what was wrong, and he softly said, "Mom, the kids at school ah making fun of me. They say I can't say my ahs vewee good."

"What should we do about it?" I asked.

"The nuse lady said my attitude is evweething. All I have to do is just pwactice." Every day for two weeks, Spencer stood in front of the mirror before and after school and worked and worked until he could say his Rs perfectly.

In the third grade, he entered competitive sports. He was ready for the ordeal – I wasn't. I thought he still looked newly hatched and terribly vulnerable. "Today I have to stay after school again and practice track," he announced one day. "Why don't you come watch me?"

Of course I went. I watched, and my heart ached because he was trying so hard with such discouraging results. From birth, one leg was three inches shorter than the other, and he had great difficulty running. Consequently, he was a high jumper, who with one strong leg flung himself through the air, often landing on the bar. Although he became scratched and battered from his fifteen attempts, he relentlessly pursued his goal.

"Haven't you had enough?" I asked in a feeble attempt to protect him from further failure. With tears in his eyes he softly answered, "The kids make fun of me and say I'm not too good at track, but the coach said I can't quit; it's a league rule."

On the next try, he succeeded in clearing the bar. At the end of the track season, I thought he had had enough last-place finishes to last a lifetime. To the contrary, he excitedly proposed, "I think I'll try out for the Little League baseball team. Maybe I'm good at baseball." He wasn't. Not only could he not run, but he couldn't see the ball. He wore thick Coke-bottle glasses.

Each evening, he returned to me exhausted, never complaining about what he couldn't do. He was tired but always had a smile.

"I missed every fly that came my way," he said one night.

"That's too bad," I sympathized. I put a comforting hand on his shoulder and noticed several bruises on his chest. "What are these spots?" I asked. He looked down. "Oh those. That's where the ball hit me."

"My goodness! Shouldn't you duck when you're about to get hit?" His eyes widened, saddened. "Mom, I wasn't supposed to get hit." "Why didn't you catch it?" I persisted.

Spencer's countenance changed and his head dropped. "That's what I was trying to do."

That night I cried myself to sleep, wondering if and when he would ever really succeed. The next day I picked him up from practice, and he had his new uniform. He ran to the car with the blue and gold jersey slung over his shoulder and a smile that lit up his face like a Christmas tree.

"I got a uniform," he announced. "There were only twelve of them. Most guys didn't get one. This was the last uniform, and the coach gave it to me. He said I'd earned it."

"Way to go," I said. It was wonderful to see him so happy. The bench warming period began after that, and although he never missed a practice or a game, I lost interest. Rationalizing that I had something better to do than just sit on a hard bleacher and watch my son sit there, I stopped going. Spencer pleaded for me to cancel my Friday evening date and come to his final game.

I arrived late but still in time to see him play. I guess his persistence had finally gotten to the coach and he put him in. In the sixth inning, which was the second to the last inning, the ball was hit his way. Spencer hobbled as fast as he could but missed it. Three more times he missed it, and the other team started catching up.

Then when it was his turn to bat, he struck out. Each mistake was announced over the loudspeaker. I was mortified and embarrassed, but somehow Spencer was not. After his poor performance, I thought for sure Spencer would be pulled from the game. It was close, and they needed a victory to win the championship. To everyone's surprise, the coach yelled to the end of the bench, "Williams, you're back in."

As Spencer walked past the bleachers, he looked up at me and the other parents and, with his patented positivity assuredly cautioned, "Whoa, Mom, we are only ahead by one run and I don't know if even I can hold them off with only one inning to play!"

We laughed. He was dead serious! No one seemed to worry, though, because this time, Spencer was put in right field where no balls had been hit all game long. There were two quick hits with the winning run now on first base. Then two quick outs. The third hit came Spencer's way. I saw the coach wince and cover his eyes. The ball sailed right into Spencer's glove. We stood to cheer until he collided with another player. He lay motionless. The other player got up and screamed that Spencer's nose was gushing blood. "I think he's dead!" he shouted. "You'd better come quick."

With the apparent winning run crossing home plate and the ballpark hushed in concerned silence, the coach jogged his way out of the dugout to administer first aid. But before he could get to him Spencer suddenly raised his hand in the air. The ball had stayed in his glove. The umpire yelled, "You're out," and our bleachers erupted into a long-cheering, standing ovation. Spencer's team had won the game!

The coach stopped walking. He couldn't believe it. No one could. With tears in his eyes, he proudly started to clap. Then in a spontaneous eruption of sportsmanship, the other team started to clap. Although they had just lost the game, one by one the opposing team members stood. Within a minute, the other fans, the two umpires, the other team's coaches, and every player on both teams were on their feet cheering for this eight-year-old hero.

My Spencer is now thirteen years old. It has been five years since that amazing day, and I've never missed another one of his extracurricular activities. In fact, I've stopped procrastinating, changed my previous life perception from half empty to half full, stopped whining about my job layoff, got more education and training, which landed me more fulfilling employment in a new job, and have never missed another day of work or a day at the gym since then. How could I when I now know that "Attitude Is Everything!"

CHAPTER NINE

"FEEDBACK" - THE BREAKFAST OF CHAMPIONS

If the wrong questions lead to confirmation bias, which leads us away from whole truth, then continual, real-time, up-to-the-minute feedback brings us that much closer. Feedback is the breakfast of champions, telling us more of the truth so we can adjust our actions.

When NASA launched a rocket to the moon, feedback determined its direction and destination. When the rocket went off course, astronauts heard beeps and either electronically or manually corrected the course.

Question: What would happen if NASA launched the rocket and waited ninety days to check up on it, as some do in the corporate world with their quarterly reports?

We all know that the quicker we recognize weakness, mediocrity, misdirection, or failure, the easier and more cost effective it is to fix it, change it, and get ourselves back on track toward our desired destination.

We stand accountable not only for what we do but also for what we don't do. And what matters is not only what we know but also what we don't know.

THREE FORMS OF FEEDBACK

By increasing how often we receive feedback, we are not only able to change our behavior, but we can also pick the most appropriate behavior to positively affect the outcome of a task, event, or game.

Feedback in all its forms gives us real-time Whole Truth that confronts us with the clear choices we face; then it's up to us to make the right decision. If our goal is significance, no one form of feedback will suffice because no single form on its own will yield the Whole Truth.

FACTUAL feedback constitutes the cold, hard facts of our current reality, data to which we assign accountability without blame.

MOTIVATIONAL feedback is the cheering crowd and encouraging coach who tells us, "You can do it—go for it!" We need motivational feedback to get us to hustle; it triggers the adrenaline and endorphins we need to dig deep and compete. Motivational feedback must not only celebrate excellence and winning, it must also celebrate improvement, which stimulates more improvement.

EDUCATIONAL feedback is correctional coaching that changes and improves or betters our job performance at work. It's also the teacher telling the child, "I love the way you attempted this math problem, but this is the change you must understand and implement to get the correct and desired answer."

Compare two winter Olympic events that often take place on the same ice rink— figure skating and ice hockey.

FIGURE SKATING FEEDBACK

During the Olympic Winter Games in Salt Lake City in 2002, I served on the Olympic Committee and attended the pairs figure skating finals. Two skaters emerged from backstage, smiling and holding hands as their names came over the PA system and skated to their places in the center of the ice. When the music began they skated their hearts out and executed their well-rehearsed beautiful spinning, leaping, elegant, and graceful four-minute routine until the last beat of the song.

As they concluded their performance, the audience gave an appreciative, polite, sophisticated applause, but then waited in dead silence. "How did they do?" I asked the stranger sitting next to him.

"Don't know yet," she said.

"The scorers' table hasn't flashed the judges' scores yet," the woman explained.

I was baffled. Everyone had watched a routine for four minutes and didn't even know what they just saw! (How many of us sit at our desks at the end of a workday with the same shocked, puzzled, deer-in-the-headlights look, wondering what happened?)

As two more minutes of waiting passed, images of the two skaters sitting in the "kiss-and-cry" area flashed up on the arena's Jumbotron.

They held hands, out of breath and sweating, while a sportscaster interviewed them. Finally the scorers' table flashed the judges' scores. Because they were much lower than the pair had prepared for, tears flowed because the skaters were devastated.

What a tragedy. All those thousands of hours, all those years of training, for this letdown. Their dreams of world championships and Olympic gold had slipped away. The score-keeping system had no way to adapt or adjust during the performance.

Although most professional skaters can intuit for themselves roughly how they are doing in the moment, the all-important formal feedback measurement came at the end of the task, when it was too late to change anything.

ICE HOCKEY FEEDBACK

The next day, I attended the gold medal ice hockey game. What a difference! While figure skating has no feedback, in hockey, everybody—the fans, the coaches, and especially the players—can see the scoreboard and know at all times the score and the time remaining.

In fact, because the feedback is constant and dynamic, it emotionally affects everybody playing and watching. At the slightest sneer, smirk, or cheap shot, the players drop their gloves to rearrange one another's faces. A lawsuit was recently filed in New York because two fans climbed over the glass and beat up the opposing team's coach.

Clearly, ice hockey is the number one cause of prison riots in North America. When inmates watch hockey on TV, they become uncontrollably mad when they see a hockey player get a five-minute penalty for the exact same offense they are doing seventeen years for! I pulled out my pad and jotted down his observation:

**Increasing our frequency of feedback allows us
to change our behavior before it is too late!**

If a team is losing by a goal with a minute left, the coach doesn't quit and give up. Instead, he adjusts, takes out the goalkeeper, and puts in a sixth attacker to tie up the game and send it into overtime.

In business management, we can't afford to wait until the quarterly report comes out in April to learn how we did in January and February. In sales, we can't afford to wait until the end of the month to learn how our totals-versus-quota ratios tallied.

In family life, parents can't wait until a child is eighteen to keep him or her off drugs and offer feedback that teaches their child about sexuality and moral responsibility. We need whole truth—as best as we can apprehend it—at all times.

Why is it so difficult for so many to understand that it's better to build a fence at the edge of a cliff than to park an ambulance at its base? It's better to prepare and prevent than to repair and repent!

We must stop and ask ourselves both professionally and personally: Is my system of measurement feedback more like figure skating or ice hockey? Do I know what's going on at all times—the whole truth—so I can quickly make essential choices along the way? Or is change, positive and especially negative, always a surprise?

BASKETBALL FEEDBACK

Making the right decision at the right time for the right reason is always predicated on receiving whole truth through timely feedback. I witnessed this during a college basketball game where the teams had gone back and forth, changing leads the entire evening.

When only three seconds remained in the game, one team was behind by one point and called a final time-out.

Then the whistle blew and play resumed. A player on the team behind by one threw the ball inbounds. A second teammate caught the ball, turned, and shot. The ball was airborne when the buzzer sounded. The game ended as the ball ripped through the net for the win. The team down by one had won by two!

Wait a minute. Why? How? Pandemonium erupted. When the player caught the inbounds pass, he didn't turn, sprint up the court, and take a short jump shot. He turned and threw the ball like a baseball the whole length of the court to the other basket—ninety feet away! Talk about a three-pointer!

Question: Because that's a totally crazy, low percentage shot, what would the coach have said to that player had he taken that shot in the middle of the first quarter? Most likely, "Calm down! Why don't you bounce it a couple more times before you launch another one!"

But because of his exposure to up-to-the-minute correct information, and constant, dynamic feedback, the player was able to alter his actions and behaviors and match them to the specific needs required at that specific moment to be successful in that specific circumstance.

As an aside, this hero player who made the game winning basket had missed his previous nine shots. Apparently the coach had reinforced his belief and confidence in this player with constant positive feedback throughout the entire game, especially when the team was behind, which allowed the player to rise to the occasion when it mattered the most.

I pulled out my pad again and added to my observation: In seeking the Whole Truth, we must remember:

Increasing our frequency of feedback also allows us to pick the most appropriate behavior required at that moment to help us positively influence and proactively change the eventual outcome of the task at hand.

EARTHQUAKE MIRACLE

One of the most remarkable illustrations of the advantages and power that come from increasing our frequency of feedback, knowing the Whole Truth and realizing that the Whole Truth truly does "set you free" came out of the largest natural disaster in modern history.

On December 26, 2004, a powerful earthquake struck off the coast of Indonesia, creating a deadly tsunami that killed more than 200,000 people. In one day, millions of lives were forever changed. But there was one group of people who, although their village was destroyed, did not suffer a single casualty. The reason? They knew the Whole Truth about the coming tsunami.

The Moken people live in villages on islands off the coast of Thailand and Burma (Myanmar). A society of fishermen, they depend on the sea. For hundreds and perhaps thousands of years, their ancestors have studied the ocean, and they have passed their knowledge down from father to son. They were careful to teach one thing in particular: what to do when the ocean receded. According to their traditions, when that happened, the laboon—a wave that eats people—would soon arrive.

When the elders of the village saw the dreaded signs, they shouted to everyone to run to high ground. Not everyone listened. But one old fisherman would not relent until all had left the village and climbed up the hillside.

The Moken people were fortunate in that they had a leader with conviction of the Whole Truth who warned them of what would follow. Had they not listened, most would have perished.

When we see warning signs such as anger, we should replace it with love. We should also replace stress with perseverance, prejudice with kindness, depression with service, and jealousy and possessiveness with confidence and self-worth.

What makes the story about the Moken people so significant is that even though the leader had a conviction of the Whole Truth, had the people not totally trusted him, they never would have taken action on his words.

CHAPTER TEN

THE TEN COMMITMENTS TO BUILDING A WINNING TEAM

THE MAKING OF AN "I" PLAYER

"Winning isn't something that happens suddenly on the field when the whistle blows and the crowds roar. Winning is something that builds physically and mentally every day that you train and every night that you dream."
—Emmitt Smith (NFL All-time Leading Rusher)

It's not all about team – teams lose. Whoever said it's not whether you win or lose that counts probably lost. There are companies going bankrupt as you read this, and they have a team. Yes, we've been taught, "There is no 'I' in team," but teams lose. (FYI: There is no "I" in sucks or loser or weak or last place either!) However, there are two "I's" in WINNING.

WINNING

The first "I" in winning represents Independent individual preparation – which is created with a commitment to the core values of Clarity, Character, Competence, Consistency, Competitiveness, and Contribution. Yes, this "I" is a focus on 'ME,' but in: 'Don't let me be the weak link.' This "I" player speaks of "my" team, not of "our" team, and strives to make self-mastery permanent because winning is very personal.

The second "I" in winning represents Interdependent collective collaboration, which is created with a commitment to the core values of Cause, Chemistry, Cooperation, and Conclusion. This "I" turns the ME into WE, by transforming the over used acronym T.E.A.M. - Together Everyone Achieves More, into the new, more powerful F.A.M.I.L.Y. - Forget About Me I Love You.

BOTTOM LINE

Yes. It is about team. But winning is really the only reason for assembling a team. The teams that win have the greatest number of "I" players on them who are consistently committed to continuously developing themselves for the benefit of the team.

TEAM SPORTS?

When we take the time to really analyze team sports, most of them are NOT team sports. I was watching a professional baseball game when a batter hits a long fly ball to the multimillion dollar super star left fielder who catches it underhanded, spins around to do a Michael Jackson 'moon walk' and then tosses the ball into the stands to an excited fan. Cool, right? Wrong! There were only two outs, with two runners on base who taunted the bone-headed move of the fielder and skipped around the bases to score the go-ahead runs. While the fielder was pleading with the fan to give him back the ball, his coach was cursing and his teammates were furious!

Think about this. When a batter faces the pitcher, it is a one on one duel between two individuals. If he strikes out the batter, the pitcher did it on his own. If the batter hits the ball, he did it on his own. If the infielder successfully fields the ground ball and throws it to first base. he did it on his own. If there is a runner on first base and the batter hits it to the shortstop, who throws it to the second baseman, he did it on his own. If the second baseman touches the base and throws it to first base to get the 'double play' out, he did it on his own. Baseball is an individual sport, played by nine individuals who must perform to the very best of their ability with the personal commitment: 'Don't let me be the weak link! Don't let me let my teammates down.'

Is soccer a team sport? When the player is dribbling the ball against a defender it is a one on one contest. When he passes the ball to another teammate it becomes a different one on one contest between him and the defender. Yes, when a player runs past his opponent, another opposing player must step up and now defend the player with the ball, but it still is a one on one competition between the player with the ball and the defender. When there is a 'corner kick' each player must do his part. It is not just a play to be made by the goalkeeper. Every teammate must do his individual part to defend the net or they will lose that point and possibly the game!

INDIVIDUAL CHAMPIONS MAKE

CHAMPIONSHIP TEAMS

Successful coaches/leaders build teams and think strictly in terms of team spirit. However, 'Significant coaches' keep in mind the greater purpose of competition, which is to win. The Art of Significant Team Building begins when the coach comprehends that it is easier to raise the performance of one leader than it is to raise the performance of a whole team. He therefore makes sure he puts into the leadership position the person who has the strength and personal courage to set the highest expectation and standard of acceptable performance required to win. This is simply achieved by focusing on the predominant strengths of that one person and the dismissal of weaknesses as irrelevant unless they hamper the aggregate strength of the team.

In other words, a significant coach knows that his/her primary task is to create an alignment of team strengths so strong that it makes the individual team member's weaknesses irrelevant.

Yes, winning takes place on the field, but all on-the-field wins originate in the individual's off-the-field commitment – in grit, determination, honor, integrity, focus, and sacrifice, where they demonstrate the level of love and respect they have for their teammates by how hard they work to stretch, raise their personal bar and jump higher than ever before – all so they can contribute more to the team.

U.S. Army General Douglas MacArthur explained it best when he said: "On the fields of friendly strife are sown the seeds that on other days, on other fields, will bear the fruits of victory. When we sweat more in peace we will bleed less in war."

For these reasons, I have taken the six core values required for Independent preparation and combined them with the four core values required for Interdependent Collaboration, to create what I call:

THE TEN COMMITMENTS TO BUILDING A WINNING TEAM

INDEPENDENT INDIVIDUAL PREPARATION

A Commitment to the First Six Cs: Clarity, Character, Competence, Consistency, Competitiveness, and Contribution

1. CLARITY

When it comes to building a winning team Clarity is divided into two tasks: creating a team identity and personality; and building that team with individuals with the required strengths to create that kind of a team. As an owner and/or coach do I want my football team to be known as an extremely physical, hard hitting, smash mouth defensive team like the Mike Singletary era Super Bowl winning Chicago Bears? Or a super athletic team with smaller more agile lineman, smaller shifty backs and receivers and an under-sized quarterback like the Joe Montana era San Fransisco 49ers whose coaching staff invented the famous "West Coast Offense" based on the unique skill set of these players?

Will I establish my basketball team identity as a run and gun high scoring offense or as a half court, slow it down and work it in, low scoring, second chance rebounding team, which dictates the kind of players I need to recruit to play in my system.

If you are a professional tennis player will you be a "baseline" player and always stay back with smooth "early preparation" ground strokes like the incredible and unique Bjorn Borg? Or will you be a "serve and volley" player like John McEnroe from that same era - both of whom were World Champions?

As a professional speaker I needed to get clear on what kind of a speaker I wanted to be and I chose to be a storyteller.

The second task in creating Clarity is personal identity. Clarity is defining who we are – personal authenticity – and knowing we must first like ourselves before we can like someone else, love ourselves before we can love someone else, and trust ourselves before we can trust someone else.

Liking, loving, and trusting yourself begins and ends with being yourself. So the primary questions in creating and sustaining clarity are: Who are you, really? What is your true calling and life's work?

Clarity is taking ownership and personal responsibility for every success and failure, knowing that success comes not from how you look or how you dress or how you're educated, but from how you think. Clarity comes when you pause and reflect, knowing perseverance and accomplishment are not long races, but rather short races one after another that we call moments of truth.

Clarity is laser-like focus that cuts through life's clutter like a powerful beacon cutting through the thick night fog. Clarity is knowing why you do what you do, and being clear on how to do it with the commitment to do what is required to take you and your teammates from where you are to where you want to be.

Once your how is clear, it illuminates what systems and processes you must put in place to ensure that the required action steps are instigated which will guarantee that your passionate why becomes a reality.

Why Are You Here?

Clarity is best understood through two titles and job descriptions that are engaged in doing the same thing, playing the same game, and fighting the same fight. The only difference between them is their motive. As explained below, mercenaries are best players; missionaries are right people; and you have to be a right human "being" before you can be a best human "doing."

We all know that most NFL players are not choirboys, but to be right for a winning team, they must at least be missionaries. Most teams are made up of mercenaries – the best hired guns motivated by money. But winning teams are made up of missionaries – the right hired hearts motivated by cause.

To be a mercenary requires nothing but an elementary, superficial mindset about yourself and your place in the world. Being a missionary requires an advanced mindset.

Mercenaries are short-term and change jobs to make money.

Missionaries are long-term and sustain careers to make a difference.

Mercenaries fight for themselves; missionaries fight for their teammates.

Mercenaries exercise blind obedience; missionaries obey because they see.

Mercenaries have eyesight, only read the lines, and if required, live the letter of the law. Missionaries have insight, read and feel in between the lines, and live the spirit of the law.

Mercenaries are obligated to no one, preach nothing, and accept no responsibility. Missionaries are obligated to something bigger than themselves and feel a responsibility to share it and live it as role models for success.

Therefore, not only do missionaries practice what they preach, but they also preach only what they practice. They constantly strive to obey and live by all of the Ten Commitments at a higher level than they did the day before.

2. CHARACTER

Every equation and journey requires that we use and follow a compass. Living with character is to meticulously measure and align your beliefs with your behavior, because if the things you think about are different from the things you do, you will never be happy or successful. Character is reputation, moral excellence, and firmness – the aggregate of distinctive qualities and ethical traits. Character spawns and perpetuates trust, which allows you to gain the confidence of others. Character is being trustworthy, loyal, obedient, thrifty, brave, clean, pure, and reverent when no one is watching.

To know and not to do is not to know at all. Do the right thing simply because it's the right thing to do, not only when people are watching, but also, and especially, when they are not.

Two friends of mine exemplify character in everything they say and do, and consequently, every time I run into them I always ask them to teach me something significant that they recently learned. Jim and Naomi Rhode own a multi-million-dollar dental supply/ consulting company that has conducted practice management seminars in Hawaii for over twenty years. One memorable encounter with them happened as I was sitting in a hot tub at my condo complex in Maui, Hawaii. Without any warning Jim and Naomi came strolling by. Excitedly we greeted one another and, as usual, I asked them what they had learned in the last few days. Naomi smiled her huge beautiful smile and explained, "Yesterday we were walking along the beach holding hands and reminiscing on the hundreds of people's lives we had touched over the years in our seminars. As we looked back we could see our footprints in the sand, which filled us with pride and we felt a sense of arrogant accomplishment. Suddenly, a huge wave crashed onto the beach, danced its whitewater dance for a few seconds, and then retreated back out to sea. My heart immediately sunk as our footprints had been swept clean from the beach, leaving no trace that we had even been there before. I immediately tied it into our seminar business and in this obvious metaphor asked Jim how we could leave our footprints in the lives of everyone we encounter in a more long-lasting impactful way? Without skipping a beat Jim replied, 'Just walk on higher ground.'"

Class

I was flying cross-country on a Boeing 757 jet, sitting in first class. I always fly first class—not because I pay for the ticket, but because I fly more than two hundred thousand miles per year on Delta Airlines and am a Diamond Medallion member (six-million miler) who automatically gets upgraded. There are twenty-four seats in first class, and I was sitting in my usual window seat.

After about two hours and five diet Cokes into the flight, I got up to use the lavatory. When I walked in and locked the door, I immediately noticed that the tiny bathroom was totally trashed. There was water everywhere, soapy slime dripping down the mirror, used paper towels on the floor, and crap on the seat. Then it hit me. The next person who comes in will immediately think I did all of this! So I started to clean it. With one hand holding my nose and doing everything I could not to throw up, I wiped the mirror and the seat, cleaned up the trash, and mopped up the floor. It was clearly one of the most appalling experiences of my life.

When I had relieved my bladder, I emerged from the lavatory and stood in front of the entire first-class section until I got eye contact with every person sitting in front of me. I was raised to be a gentleman, so I didn't say anything. But I wanted so badly to yell, "Okay, which one of you low-budget loser bums did this?"

As I sat down, I realized you cannot buy class. Sitting in first class doesn't make you first-class! You can lie to others and fake out the world, but you cannot lie to yourself.

It truly is what we do when no one is around that defines who we really are.

Remember: adversity is what introduces us to ourselves. No one will ever know how strong we are until being strong is the only choice we have. Crisis does not make or break the man or woman - it just reveals the true character within Character is doing the right thing!

3. COMPETENCE

As you recognize your inherent abilities, acquire knowledge and master technical skills, you achieve a level called competence, which is the third C in the Ten Commitments that make "I" players winners. Competence is doing things right. In sports, Competence is achieved when you memorize your team play book and know every play inside and out - knowing what every player on your team does on every play - and studying your opponent so you know his plays and strengths and weaknesses.

Competence in business is having a complete and comprehensive knowledge and understanding of your organization's products and services - with the ability to teach, present and sell your products and services with articulate and persuasive eloquence. Competence breeds respect from teammates and coworkers and confidence in your leaders and from those whom you lead.

What most people do not realize is that regardless of how great the players or employees or military personnel are, and even if they subscribe to the Ten Cs, they cannot become the "I" players we need them to be if they do not have total confidence in their coaches, leaders, and the system in which they work and live. Having complete and unquestioned confidence in competent leaders permits people to achieve unexpected high levels of performance through routines that activate talent.

Confidence

Confidence is the reason that success and failure are not mere episodes but self-perpetuating trajectories, and why organizations of all types may be brimming with talent but not be winners. Losing streaks are often created and then perpetuated when people lose confidence in their leaders and systems, while winning streaks are fueled by competent and confident people who are secure in their own abilities and the ability of their leaders. Winning streaks are characterized by continuity and continued investment, while losing streaks are marked by disruption and a lack of investment that typically give way to a self-fulfilling prophecy of failure.

Remember: "If you know the enemy and know yourself, you need not fear the result of a hundred battles. If you know yourself but not the enemy, for every victory gained you will also suffer a defeat. If you know neither the enemy nor yourself, you will succumb in every battle." -Sun Tzu

4. CONSISTENCY

Like a perfectly fit and well-oiled machine, we must perfectly practice to the point that we develop a subconscious muscle memory that is permanent, firm, steady, and free from variation or contradiction and that is always reliable, predictable, and trusted. Character, confidence, and consistency create a commitment to excellence in everything we do and welcome change as improving and becoming more of who we already are.

One of my favorite stories about consistency occurred while I attended a press conference in Hawaii at the Senior Skins Golf Game. A reporter asked the great Jack Nicklaus when his incredibly talented son was going to turn pro. Nicklaus smiled and said, "My son is a scratch golfer and, yes, he plays very well. But right now he can only concentrate for eight holes. As soon as he can concentrate and stay focused for all eighteen holes, he will be ready for the big-time challenge of the PGA Tour."

Discipline

Responsibility brings freedom and freedom provides opportunity. That's the principle of self-discipline.

Self-discipline sounds like some kind of punishment you administer to yourself. It really means you are in control of your actions and the outcome—at least to some degree.

Self-discipline means avoiding outside discipline by doing the right thing. Arabian horses are a perfect example of the kind of self-control each of us is capable of achieving.

These magnificent horses with intelligent eyes, well - formed heads, and flowing manes and tails win many championships because of their stamina and courage.

While they are all hearty specimens, some horses stand above the others for endurance and intelligence. To determine which they are, trainers teach them to drink only when they hear a whistle. Once they have learned to obey, they are placed in a corral under the hot sun until they are parched. Then water is brought and placed outside the corral out of their reach, forcing them to wait even longer.

Finally, a gate is opened, and most of them stampede for the trough to drink with reckless abandon. Only a few stand poised with pride, holding their heads erect, and don't give in to the terrible craving. Only when they hear the whistle do they allow themselves to drink. The ones who obey and resist the urge to drink are reserved for special training. The other steeds are led away.

So it is with humans. The mark of a champion is not on the outside, but somewhere deep inside, where self-control resides.

To gain control of yourself and become self-disciplined is the second step to becoming successful. First, see yourself as a conqueror. Then discipline yourself to become one.

Unfortunately, many folks who see themselves as champions are not willing to put in the extra effort and self-imposed discipline to become winners. Consequently, they lose out to those with restraint.

Ten things anyone can consistently do that require no talent:

1. Being Trustworthy
2. Being Positive
3. Being Passionate
4. Being On Time
5. Being Present
6. Being Coachable
7. Being Prepared
8. Being Hard Working
9. Being Loyal
10. Being Conscientious

5. COMPETITIVENESS

To get what you've never had, you must roll the dice and do what you've never done: cease to complain; create, adapt, transform, modify; be different without losing identity; stretch beyond the point of discomfort; find the opportunity in change; and alter your thinking, strategy, and behavior before you have to. Competition should always begin and end with our selves. Too many people think nobility comes by being superior to some other person, but true nobility actually comes only from being superior to your previous self.

You must always remember that the only person you need to be better than is the person you were yesterday! You need to be the very best version of yourself - at all times, in all places, knowing you will make a lousy somebody else!

Ask yourself: are you tall, short, fast, slow, wide, thin, smart, stupid, pretty, or pretty ugly? Says who? Compared to what? Albert Einstein said, "Everybody is a genius. But if you judge a fish by its ability to climb a tree it will spend its whole life believing that it is stupid."

If every bird in the forest sang the same tune it would be a boring forest. If every player on the football team was a cunning, fleet-of-foot quarterback or a large, super strong lineman they would not win a single game. Competitiveness must first and always begin within and against ourselves so in every practice and in every game we Make Winning Personal!

There is a reason that competing fast food restaurants occupy all four corners of the same intersection. They want to feed off of each other's traffic, but they only compete against themselves. If one of them goes out of business, it is never the other's fault. It is because of poor leadership, ineffective management, bad food, horrible customer service, filthy washrooms, and an unreasonable price. If price becomes the topic of conversation, it means the presentation is weak and the relationship is nonexistent.

When we are not the very best we can possibly be so as to differentiate ourselves from our friends and coworkers in good, clean, pure, powerful, positive ways, we are forced to compete at the lowest common denominators of price and politics, which are based on who is right instead of what is right.

Do You Shun Competition?

Competition is the economic system America is based on. Capitalism exists and thrives on this simple principle.

Mr. Ling owned a dry-cleaning store that had been in the family for years. Then a developer came along and wanted to push Mr. Ling out of his spot to make room for a new shopping mall. Mr. Ling did not know how to do anything else for a living. He didn't want to lose this store, and he made it clear to the developer he was going to stay put.

The conflict escalated as the developer built the shopping mall around Mr. Ling's establishment. To get even, the developer put dry-cleaning shops on both sides of Mr. Ling to drive him out of business. Most would have quit, but not Mr. Ling.

The Ling family hadn't been in business for so many years without knowing how to compete and survive. To combat the competition, Mr. Ling made a giant sign and hung it above the entrance of his store. After he hung the sign, Mr. Ling had more business than ever. What did the sign say? THIS WAY TO MAIN ENTRANCE.

There is always a way to survive. When we rise to the level of our competition, we become better.

Like Mr. Ling, you might find it hard, but only those who compete are going to survive, thrive, and succeed.

6. CONTRIBUTION

Contributing is using every tool in your toolbox to give it everything you've got when less would be sufficient; being fully alive; serving, participating, supporting, supplying; playing a significant part in bringing about an end or result; doing what is expected and then some; meeting your requirements and responsibilities fairly and squarely and then some; being helpful, friendly, courteous, kind, and counted on in an emergency and then some.

Ralph Waldo Emerson wrote, "It is one of the most beautiful compensations in life – we can never help another without helping ourselves." Because we coach behavior, not results, contribution is the way we behave our way to significance. Total contribution breeds and sustains trust. First, our trust in ourselves, and second, our teammates' trust, because we are giving maximum effort with a consistent willingness to help in all situations without ever saying, "It's not my job."

Contribution is making suggestions for improvement, which applies not only to an employee or player bringing a problem to a manager or coach, but also to an employer or coach giving feedback to an employee or player, a teacher to a student, a parent to a child, a coworker to a coworker, and a friend to a friend. If you have thought enough to recognize that a problem exists, you have the responsibility to also turn the problem into a positive-growth challenge by providing a possible solution.

This is the difference between complainers, whiners, and cancerous negative discontents, and an "I" player who truly wants to personally and collectively get better and positively contribute as a problem-solving, possibility-thinking ally.

Commitment to total contribution is realizing that victory is always the goal, which inspires us to dig deeper when necessary and rise to the occasion by hustling to give that something more – physically, mentally, and emotionally.

Big Time 'I' Players, Come Up Big, In Big Time Games

One of the greatest single examples of why and how the combination of Clarity, Character, Competence/Confidence, Competitiveness, Cause, and Chemistry guarantee Consistent peak performance, especially when the game is on the line, was illuminated during the 1988 World Series rivalry match between the Oakland Athletics and the Los Angeles Dodgers. Although five games were played, the Series is remembered because of one pinch-hit walk-off home run, which ultimately led to the Dodgers upsetting the heavily favored A's to win the Series.

On paper both teams were relatively equal on the mound. However, the A's held a slight advantage at the plate after assembling the "Dynamic Duo" of Jose Canseco and Mark McGwire who combined for seventy- four home runs and two-hundred twenty-three runs batted in during the regular season. With such evenly matched teams, sports commentators proposed this West Coast vs. West Coast affair would go to seven games. My oh my were they surprised!

It was game one at Dodger Stadium and very few experts gave LA a chance to win because their MVP super star slugger Kirk Gibson could barely walk due to injuries suffered during the National League Championship Series. With two swollen knees and a nagging hamstring injury Gibson wasn't even introduced before the game. Too hurt to play, Gibson reluctantly stayed in the locker room receiving physical therapy and treatment while watching the game on TV.

Suddenly the phone on the wall rang and Coach/Manager Tommy Lasorda asked Kirk to come up to the field to pinch-hit in the bottom of the ninth inning. The Dodgers were behind 4-3 and teammate Mike Davis had just been walked. With Davis on first base and two outs, Gibson limped onto the field in a triumphant stroll that ignited Dodger fans into a crazed frenzy, believing that if anybody could save the day it would be their hero Gibson!

Hall-of-Fame Athletics pitcher Dennis Eckersley was the intimidating closer on the mound who had allowed only five home runs all year. With an injured and half-speed Gibson at bat, Oakland assumed they would be out of the inning in three pitches with a win. Sure enough, Gibson came out swinging and hit the first two pitches foul. Then took a ball. Then fouled off two more pitches and took two more balls. With a full count of three balls and two strikes, Kirk turned on the next fastball and using only his arms, miraculously hit the game winning home run deep over the right field fence. Unbelievable!

With the crowd cheering and screaming and stomping even louder than when he walked out of the dugout onto the field, Kirk threw his arm in the air, hobbled to first base, gave a double fist pump as he rounded second, and was mobbed by Coach Lasorda and teammates when he touched home base! Game over. Oakland could never recover from this shocking demoralizing loss and the Dodgers went on to win this World Series four games to one!

Kirk Gibson will be forever known as THE 'I' Player, who with Clarity and Character, was Consistently Competent enough to Compete against himself with a shared Cause that drove him to Contribute with positive contagious Chemistry, and rise to the occasion to win the game for his teammates, coaches, fans and himself.

Contribution Builds and Sustains Trust

Using the "broomstick analogy," if your teammates know you can jump 24 inches high, and you only contribute a minimum effort by jumping twelve inches high, they don't trust you. The Whole Truth then takes center stage, and no one wants you on his or her team.

And if you are on the team, when the contest or battle begins, you weaken the cooperative effort to win because the teammate next to you doesn't trust you to execute your job, so he believes he must do your job for you.

When he has to do two jobs (one of which he has not practiced), his performance is weakened, and he becomes the weak link!

Unselfishness

A powerful example of unselfish contribution took place during the 1999 NFL football season when Buffalo Bills fullback Sam Gash wanted to carry the ball and rack up individual statistics that would ultimately equate to more money in his next contract negotiation. However, in the offensive system the Bills were running, Gash was required to be the designated blocking back. Most football players of his caliber would have balked and complained about this coaching request, but Gash put his selfish agenda aside and earned the unique distinction as the first and only running back in NFL history to be selected to the Pro Bowl without carrying the ball even one time during the season.

Do What You Can Do

What you love to do reveals itself as you stop letting what you cannot do interfere with what you can do, and focus on the one thing you can become successful and significant at doing. Master martial artist Bruce Lee said, "I fear not the man who has practiced 10,000 kicks once. I fear the man who has practiced one kick 10,000 times."

So what's holding you back? The greatest mistake you can make in life is to continually fear you will make one. Yes, the start is what stops most people; yes, it takes courage to grow up and become who you really are. However, when you realize you can't always control what happens, but you can always control what happens next, and take a chance on doing just once what others say you can't do, you will never pay attention to their limitations again. Remember: every time you stay out late; every time you sleep in; every time you miss a workout; every time you don't give 100 percent, you make it that much easier for me to beat you—not because I'm bigger, faster, stronger, and smarter but because you have already beaten yourself.

"If a man is called to be a street sweeper, he should sweep streets even as Michelangelo painted, or Beethoven composed music, or Shakespeare wrote poetry. He should sweep streets so well that all the hosts of heaven and earth will pause to say, 'Here lived a great street sweeper who did his job well."
—Dr. Martin Luther King Jr.

CHAPTER ELEVEN

INTERDEPENDENT COLLECTIVE COLLABORATION OF THE TEN COMMITMENTS TO BUILDING A WINNING TEAM

(CONTINUATION)

A Commitment to the Last Four Cs:
Cause, Chemistry, Cooperation, and Conclusion

7. CAUSE

The earth is a self -contained, interdependent, inter-connected system of people, places, and things that presents a challenge for each of us to discover why and where we fit into this global interaction. Identifying our specific purpose and why we do what we do identifies the cause that makes winning personal and sows the seed that brings forth good fruit revealed by how we do it.

Cause is the principle or movement militantly defended or supported that allows you to leave your family, friends, coworkers, teammates, and the world in better shape than you found them. We should all be familiar with the following Bible verse: "Where there is no vision, the people perish" (Proverbs

29:18). Vision can be defined as the clearly quantified big picture, the most valuable long-term result that can be achieved.

To get the competitive advantage in war, you need nighttime vision; in medicine you need X- ray vision; in leadership you need Superman vision that allows you to see through the outside walls of people and look into their soul. What allows us to do this is sharing our vision in the context of a common cause and seeing who agrees and follows us. Those who do are the "I" players who will stay by our side and fight until we win.

When Our 'Cause' Is Bigger Than Our Selves

For those of us who have seen the earth from space, the experience teaches us that the things we share in our world are far more valuable than those that divide us. No longer should we talk about "cultural diversity" and what makes us different. Life and leadership are about comprehending and perpetuating "cultural commonality" and what makes us the same. More than ever before I now realize:

Every man's heart will one day beat its final beat. His lungs will breathe their final breath. And if what that man did in his life makes the blood pulse through the body of others and makes them believe deeper in something larger than life, then his essence and spirit will be immortalized by the loyalty of those who honor him, revere him as a relentless warrior for what matters most, and remember him as one who stirred the souls of men to be what they could be.

Everyone surely dies, but not everyone truly lives! Those who die before they're dead are prisoners of the past. Those who are fully alive are pioneers of the future, who have found their calling in fueling the fire of those who desire to turn their miniature dream into a mighty reality - allowing them to leave a legacy of leadership and love that will never die!

The planet doesn't need more successful people who only want to change themselves. The planet needs more revolutionaries who challenge the status quo and blaze a trail less traveled that spawns more peacemakers, healers, restorers, lovers, storytellers, and significant human beings who are crazy enough to believe we can change the world!

This is what it means to find your 'calling.' This is what it means to find your passionate purpose and life's work. This is what it happens when you buy into a 'Cause' that will help you leave a legacy of love, sacrifice, hard work, discipline, focus and winning championships behind!

Bottom line: When your "why" includes you as the end in mind, you become more passionate, creative, imaginative, resourceful, and motivated to turn your patience into perseverance and not let what you cannot do interfere with what you can do, especially in becoming everything you were born to be!

In football and in every other sport, once the game starts the coach has to stay on the sideline. So the question on the field, floor or court is: "Who is going to make a play? Who is going to step up and 're-obligate' him/her self to do whatever is necessary in that moment for the greater 'Cause?'"

"No one has ever become poor by giving. Nor is there any exercise better for the heart than reaching down and lifting people up. The simplest acts of kindness are by far more powerful than a thousand heads bowing in prayer."
—Mahatma Gandhi

8. CHEMISTRY

Under a microscope, chemistry is the people-building business of creating a winning team joined in a common cause by elements that generate contagious, strong, mutual attraction and attachment. It's vibes that make the relationship click, where everybody says in the purest form of cohesion, "I like me best when I'm with you; I want to see you again."

Chemistry is not discovered; it is created with an individual positive attitude toward our team members by going out of our way to be liked and appreciated by our peers. Although clarifying the cause, individually and collectively as a team, is the starting place for building a winning team and sustaining a winning streak, without chemistry, nothing of a long-term nature will ever exist or sustain itself.

Everybody wants to win, and every coach and player, employer and employee, usually shares that vision. Cause is easy to inspire.

However, we must remember that a lot of teams have a lot of very expensive highly paid "I" players who want to win, but still don't win. Why? They have cause, but they lack the right chemistry to support that cause.

We must remember that chemistry works hand in glove with cause and cooperation in making everybody else around you feel they are needed, part of a family, and better because they are playing side by side with you. The NBA is filled with "best" players who have four or five Cs, like former superstar Alan Iverson, who is committed to clarity – he knows he is selfish and self-centered; competence – he can shoot and score; consistency – game after game you can count on him to shoot forty shots to get his thirty points; and competitiveness – he goes full speed in games but not in practice because "it's only practice!" But to be a right player who takes everyone to the next level, not just the teammates he is playing with but the players on the opposing team he is playing against, he must possess all Ten Commitments.

Losing even one "I" player on a team or one "I" employee in a company affects team chemistry, and unless you can get it back (not with the best but with the right people), taking your organization to the ultimate level, becoming more of who you are, and consistently winning is only wishful thinking.

Leaders Are Chemists

The right coaches, corporate executives, and military leaders use their influence to brew a perfect blend of talent, skill, knowledge, personality, attitude, commitment, and other best ingredients into the right concoction to win the game. The quality of the ingredients always determines the quality of the end result of a winning or losing team, a delicious or disgusting cake! Carl Jung wrote, "The meeting of two personalities is like the contact of two chemical substances; if there is any reaction, both are transformed." Atomic reaction epitomizes these words because it can serve as either positive power or destructive control.

Because this is true in every personal, marital, significant other, family, and coworker relationship or interaction, having the right chemistry to create the right reaction is key to creating a winning team.

Therefore, the coach – or executive leader – in charge of assembling the right chemical mix of players must be more than smart. The coach must be wise about what we have already illustrated.

Chemistry really does matter. You can assemble all the best chemicals, but if they are not the right chemicals, the reaction can be disastrous. A right player or person is much more valuable than one of the best. Winners are right, and only right players consistently win.

Elevator Gas

On a more humorous but equally disgusting note, when we landed, I checked into my hotel and went to bed. The next morning, I boarded the elevator on the twentieth floor to go downstairs to the ballroom to speak to thirty-five hundred people attending the general session of a convention. I was on the elevator alone until it stopped on the fifteenth floor. On walked a large man dressed in an expensive suit. As soon as the doors shut, he passed gas in a long, loud, offensive way. I couldn't believe it! He looked sophisticated on the outside, but he lacked couth on the inside!

Then, wouldn't you know it? He got off on the very next floor, leaving just as it started to smell. My eyes were watering and my saliva dried up. I've hit skunks on the road that smelled better. Then, "ding," the elevator doors opened on the tenth floor, and eight people with conference nametags hanging around their necks got on. They were going to be in my audience, and every one of them was staring at me in disgust, thinking I was the skunk.

I wanted to explain and tell them what had happened, but I couldn't. In this case, it's more truth than humor that rank character can linger a long time. There's something to be said about leaving a positive legacy and taking pride in how we will be remembered after we are gone.

THE COST OF NOT HAVING 'I' PLAYERS

Have you ever added up the cost to an organization when only 50 percent of the employees love their jobs because the other 50 percent doesn't respect their incompetent manager/leader and are not inspired by their coworkers?

Have you ever considered the price an organization pays when only 50 percent of its people are self-starters? And less than a fourth follow a structured self-development program to better themselves wherein they set meaningful goals, prioritize their time, seek professional growth opportunities, and consequently view their employment as a job rather than a career?

The bad news is that the cost is way too high, and with lack of focus, misaligned individual agendas, conflicting purposes, poor communication, and lack of trust, eventually the organization loses so much money it is forced to close its doors.

The good news is that because a chain is only as strong as its weakest link, when we eliminate the weak links, or better still, inspire and train the weak links to strengthen themselves through accelerated and sustained intense personal effort, any team can be transformed into a high-performing, efficient, effective, significant winning team, one link, one person at a time.

Remember, we don't win with the best players/employees. We win and create a dynasty organization that keeps winning the championship with the right people!

Successful "Best" Players Practice Until They Get Better.
Significant "Right" Players Practice Until They Don't Miss!

"Chemistry cannot emerge unless each individual moves beyond ego, jealousy, and possessiveness, realizing that doing so is necessary if we ourselves are to flourish as human beings. Chemistry means opening our hearts and minds to our teammates, seeing ourselves in them and them in us, and growing in the process into our best selves." —Dan Clark

9. COOPERATION (AND COLLABORATION)

A calculator shows us that each and every entry matters to the sum total. The same is true when it comes to building a winning team. Significant leaders solicit individual entries to create the required equation that adds up to the final calculated consensus from the team. Because everyone feels valued and relevant, everyone realizes that disagreement is not a weapon. It's a communication tool, which means the leader never eliminates conflict but rather manages it.

True and effective leaders realize that the success and significance of a team is only a reflection of the people on the team, and if they have a team that underperforms, it's because they are underperforming leaders.

A.R.T. Awareness, Refinement, Transformation

As coaches become Aware of this and commit to Refining their attitudes and cooperative collaboration skills, the Transformation in this Cycle of ART begins when they fully understand the difference between an emotion and a need – especially when they are faced with a disagreement within the team.

Disagreements are obviously emotional, and every emotion is being driven by a need. Therefore, we don't talk to feelings (which is 30 percent of the disagreement); we address only the need (which is 70 percent and the cause of the disagreement).

Attempting to fix feelings is a no-win proposition that confuses activity with accomplishment. However, all of us can address and satisfy each other's needs in every team-building assignment when we take the time to understand the practical application and rules of cooperation and collaboration.

Together, cooperation and collaboration mean common effort and a willingness and ability to successfully work for the benefit of others because you know your effort, participation, and contribution really do make a difference.

Cooperation and collaboration constantly emphasize through word and deed that we are one – that we live together and die together. A teammate struggles, and you help; a door needs to be opened, and you open it; a piece of trash is in your path, and you pick it up; a job needs to be completed, and you do it.

Cooperation and collaboration are the hybrid practical application of chemistry. In basketball, for example, if you are an extraordinary shooter and scorer, you are likely always double-teamed. So you become an extraordinary passer and concentrate your energy more on playing tenacious defense for the greater good of the team.

"No one is an island; everyone is connected to someone and something that requires mutual trust and inspiration, not intimidation or domination. If I have seen further, it is by standing on the shoulders of giants." —Isaac Newton

10. CONCLUSION

Focus and Finish. Anybody can run a race. The object is to win. In sales, anybody can make a presentation. The objective is to close the deal. There is a huge difference between training to fight, and training to win! As an 'I' player you must first commit to making winning personal. Only then can you put your very best, most prepared version of yourself forward in a team setting to help others also 'focus and finish.'

Committing to live by this tenth and final 'C' Commitment, means you have the same level of mental toughness and intestinal fortitude as a world class athlete has in his individual sport.

Desire

Desire is an extraordinary, intense determination. It is a fighting heart with a burning commitment to a cause. This desire burns through in the field of athletic competition—where struggle is fierce and perseverance is profound. Sports competition is life personified.

To be successful in life, you must think like sports champions think: they believe they can run faster, jump higher, and throw farther than anyone else. That's why they continue to break world records. They understand desire, and they are willing to fight for it, regardless of the situation.

Losing Focus And Regaining Focus To Finish

The year was 1987, when U.S. speed skater Dan Jansen's sister Jane, who was also a speed skater, was diagnosed with leukemia. Inspired by her relentless battle to live, Dan won three gold medals at the World Championships held in Milwaukee just two weeks before the 1988 Calgary Olympic Games.

But seven hours before the biggest race of his career, Dan received word that his sweet sister had passed away. Despite his inconceivable sorrow, he resolved he would win for Jane, determined to live up to everyone's expectations and capture the gold.

Lining up for the 500-meter sprint against Japan's Yasushi Kuroiwa, Jansen adjusted the hood on his sleek racing suit and took a deep breath. Clearly his body was there but not his mind or his heart. "Don't wish it was easier; wish you were better. If you are not willing to risk the unusual, you will have to settle for the ordinary. The few who do are the envy of the many who only watch."

Of course, he busted out of the starting blocks, but in the first turn suddenly and shockingly fell and skidded violently into the padded wall—a heartbreaking scene of agony. With the world watching, he slowly rose from the ice and skated toward the side of the oval. Feeling he had let his sister down, he buried his face in his hands.

In the following 1000-meter race he fell again. In 1992, at Albertville, France, he placed fourth in the 500-meter and an embarrassing twenty-sixth in the 1000-meter. Despite these disappointments, Jansen continued to persevere and stretch himself in his training, retaining his place on the U.S. Olympic team for the 1994 games.

In the 500-meter race, he slipped momentarily, avoiding a fall but losing enough time to wind up in eighth place. In the 1000-meter race, his last Olympic event and his last race ever, Jansen finally won a gold medal, establishing a world-record time of 1 minute 12.43 seconds.

Jansen's coach, Dr. Jim Loehr, revealed that the reason Dan was finally able to win that elusive Olympic gold was that he had developed an emotional focus on the moment. Jim convinced Dan that thinking about winning for his sister, or dwelling on the fact that it was his last race and final opportunity to win an Olympic medal, was counterproductive and would drain his energy and detract from his focus.

All Jansen needed to do was to focus his stretch on "right now" and on each subsequent "right now," needing to persevere only one moment at a time. Technically, it was "one foot in front of the other." Mentally, it was to "maintain feelings of gratitude for all the years the sport had given him."

Tennis Tenacity

Ranked #1 in the world as a legendary tennis super star, Roger Federer had already won 21 Grand Slam titles in his career, and had won nine Wimbledon titles as the reigning perennial champion. However, in the 2018 quarterfinal match against eighth seeded Kevin Anderson, top seeded Federer finally met his match - not only physically, but mentally and emotionally. In front of a 'pro Federer' audience, Kevin proved true that 'No Pain No Gain' really means 'No Heart No Chance!'

"Down two-sets-to-love the only thing I could do was keep fighting," said the 32-year-old Anderson, playing in his first Wimbledon quarterfinal. "I just kept telling myself today was going to be my day. Today, one shot at a time, will be my payoff for training and working so hard."

Federer, who held a match point in the 10th game of the third set, was sent packing in dramatic fashion by Anderson in a 4-hour, 14-minute quarterfinal marathon match that scored 2-6, 6-7 (5), 7-5, 6-4, 13-11.

It marked only the third time in his entire career that Anderson has rebounded from a two-sets deficit to win a five-set match and he did it at Wimbledon against the highly favored Federer. In their previous four meetings, Anderson had never won a set.

Federer, long anointed the 'king of grass courts,' handed Anderson the match on his serve in the 23rd game of the fifth set when Federer double-faulted at 30-30 for the first time in the match, and only fourth time in the tournament. This gave Anderson the first break point of the final set. At 30-40, Federer netted a forehand to surrender his serve, which cost him the match.

"As the match went on, Anderson kept getting stronger and more creative and I couldn't surprise him anymore," said Federer, reflecting on what went wrong. "I couldn't come up with enough good stuff for him to miss more. It was as if something was ignited deep inside him that gave him an edge. I think that was the key at the end."

At 40-15 in the final game, Anderson hit a forehand winner to end Federer's dream of another Wimbledon trophy. Yes, Anderson served 28 aces and scored 65 winners to 61 for Federer, but at the end of the day it boiled down to who wanted it more. When asked what the difference was in his play today compared to playing Federer on previous occasions in other tournaments Anderson concluded, "Today was an emotional victory and breakthrough day for me because after the first two disastrous sets, my pride and purpose and desire over powered the self-imposed intimidation that I had believed about Federer being unbeatable. So I stopped thinking and let my instincts and desire take over, which generated energy and confidence enough for me to refuse to lose!"

Never Underestimate The Power Of
A Fighting Heart And A Burning Desire

After such an emotionally draining and physically exhausting performance in this quarterfinal match, not many fans and none of the television commentators gave Anderson a chance to win his next semifinal match the following day. However, Anderson surprised his critics by showing up with the same 'go for broke' attitude and mental toughness he had the day before and beat John Isner 7-6 (6), 6-7 (5), 6-7 (9), 6-4, 26-24 in a marathon between two big servers that lasted more than 6.5 hours.

The fifth set alone lasted nearly 3 hours, as this semifinal became a test of heart, desire, extra effort, and second wind endurance, which required the perfect mixture of 'will' and skill. In an acrobatic display of determination and grit, Anderson finally earned the must-have, go-ahead service break with the help of a point in which the right-hander tumbled to his backside, scrambled back to his feet and hit an unbelievable shot with his left hand!

Because of these intangible qualities and attributes, Anderson won the longest Centre Court match in history and earned a chance to compete for his first Grand Slam championship in Sunday's finals. Unfortunately, he lost Wimbledon to the better play of Novak Djokovic.

Conclusion In A Team Setting

The end result of living by the first nine Cs is the creation of a team in which every coach is loyal to every other coach, every player is loyal to every other player, and every coach and player is loyal to each other — all for the sake of wining the same trophy. They are loyal to those who are not present, never backbiting or gossiping about one another. And they know that through loyalty they W-I-N, focusing on What's Important Now until they achieve their desired result.

Loyalty

Loyalty is usually defined as a noun: "something to which one is bound by a pledge or duty." I disagree. I think of loyalty as an action verb that sustains the team to conclude what it started. Conclusion means perseverance; honest realistic optimism to endure no matter what; knowing that if we will spend an extra hour each day studying our chosen field or position of expertise, we will soon become an expert in that field or position!

Unity

The results of living by the previous nine Cs also reveal that chemistry with a cause, and competence with confidence, creates unity. And only with unity and through unity can you build a winning team.

The key to a unified team is a unified soul — one that is at peace with itself and not given to inner conflicts and tensions. Unity is about harmony and comes only through humility. It is the residual effect of people with a common cause bound together in reverent, respectful interdependence. Unity comes through unconditional love and is that sense of oneness wherein if one wins we all win, when one loses we all lose, when one laughs or cries we all laugh and cry together.

While divisiveness, faultfinding, antagonism, and jealousies in the hearts of teammates slowly erode team chemistry, it is backbiting and gossip that quickly destroy the team. When someone talks negatively about another person who is not present, we should always wonder what that person will say about us when we are not present. The good news is that unity can be created at every level, in every organization, to help build a winning team.

Unity Through Strength In Diversity

(The following story was told to me by former NFL superstar quarterback and former U.S. Congressman Jack Kemp. In his own words):

"In 1961, when I was quarterback and captain of the San Diego Chargers, we were scheduled to play the Houston Oilers at their home field for the AFL Championship. Traditionally, the night before the game, coach Sid Gilman took the entire team to a movie. Shortly after we sat down in our seats, I noticed that Paul Lowe, Ernie Wright, Ernie Ladd and Charlie McNeil were missing. I asked around and discovered they had been sent to the "blacks -only" balcony. When I told Coach Gilman, he stood immediately and said, 'Gather the team. Get all the guys. We're outa here.' In a silent, but powerful demonstration of our belief in equality, living and working as a team, we walked out as a team. I was proud of Coach Gilman, but so much more needed to be done."

"Four years later, after I had joined the Buffalo Bills and been elected captain, we were at the 1965 AFL All-Star Game in New Orleans. Our black teammates had trouble getting a taxi or even basic service at restaurants. Here again, the wisdom of team unity, and, admittedly, the popularity of pro football, gave us the leverage needed to combat discrimination. We discussed the situation at our team meeting and agreed to boycott the game as a statement against the racial climate in the city. As a result, the game was moved to Houston, which by that time had made progress toward more equal treatment in public accommodations. This was the first boycott of a city by any professional sporting event in history.

"We didn't tolerate bigotry on the field, either. Any difference in race, creed and class immediately dissolved in the common aim of a team win. Divisiveness only weakens a team. It has no place in the huddle, on or off the field. Each team requires unity. A team has to move as one unit, one force, with each person understanding and assisting the roles of his teammates. If a team doesn't to that, whatever the reason, it goes down in defeat. You win as a team, as a family."

Jack Kemp served 18 years as a congressman for Western New York's 31st congressional district. He then became Housing Secretary in President George H.W. Bush's cabinet, where he continued to practice and share his Team Building philosophy on creating Unity through Strength In Diversity by helping those in need of housing throughout our country. Mr. Kemp passed away in 2009.

The Legacy of Memorials

Conclusion is about winning so we can leave behind a lasting positive legacy of leadership and significant accomplishment that will inspire those who follow. For example, the builders of the spectacular Washington Monument on the National Mall in Washington, D.C., gathered commemorative stones from each state of the then-unified Union and encased them within the interior of the 555-foot structure as a tribute not only to the first president and father of our country but also to our national unity.

Notice that I said the "then-unified Union" because as this world's largest masonry building was being constructed, America entered into the bloodiest internal conflict we have ever known. What the Washington Monument really symbolizes is what President Abraham Lincoln said in a Civil War speech in which, quoting the Bible, he unashamedly warned: "A house divided against itself cannot stand." Lincoln's success or failure as president hinged upon whether he could conclude the Civil War and unify the nation. Thankfully, he did!

"An American football game is one sixty-minute game but rather sixty-one-minute games, each with its own beginning and end, with a personal commitment to play every play, never taking one off, always hustling and giving it your all until the whistle blows and that play ends. So likewise is life with her countless plays and individual conclusions. Yes, conclusion means you have focused and finished but only in the mindset of a commencement graduation, which means "new beginning," where as one door shuts behind you, another one opens. Conclusion is to finish each moment, to find the journey's end in every step of the road, to live the greatest number of good hours, to live a lifetime every day, to be fully alive from the moment you awake to the second you fall fast asleep, until you conclude your slumber and rise again to take your next first step on your journey in the new day." —Dan Clark

NO COMPROMISE

Notice I have not mentioned compromise as one of the Ten Commitments To Building A Winning Team. Compromise has no place in building a winning team. In sports, we know that momentum lasts only as long as your next play, and that once you experience a momentum shifter (like a blocked kick or a goal-line stand), what you do on the very next play allows you to take advantage of this newly captured momentum. Why would anyone want to give up this competitive advantage just to make it fair and make sure no one feels bad so they keep playing the game?

We normally negotiate a compromise on a linear plane: You give up something and I give up something, and we meet in the middle, weaker than we were by ourselves, just so we can stay together.

It's like the second law of thermodynamics: you put a hot substance in the same vat with a cold substance, and within minutes they reach an average warm temperature. Even more problematic, compromise is about who is right and holding onto whatever you can. Are you kidding me? I thought change and winning were not about who is best, but about what is right. Significant people obey higher, universal laws whether it's in their selfish interest or not. Do we merely live by situational ethics, selective integrity, service for self, and excellence in only a few things we do? Absurd!

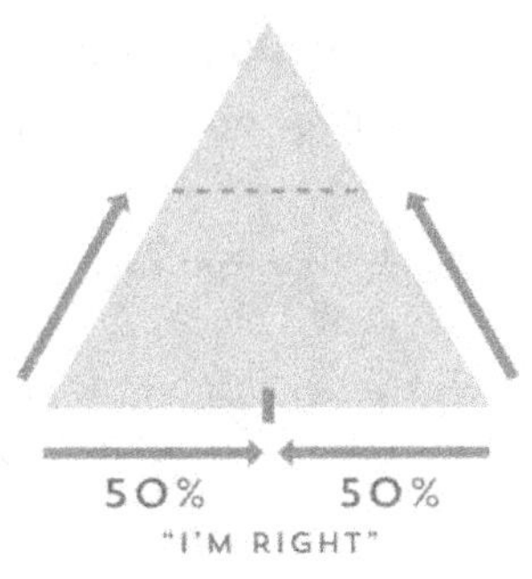

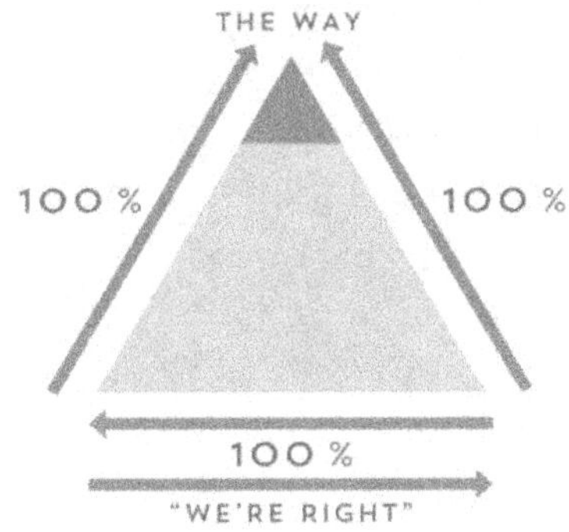

Zen Buddhists never compromise and they are the most peace-loving people on our planet. They envision negotiating as an equilateral triangle, where each party begins at one end of the base and moves upward toward the triangle's apex. Moving closer and closer to becoming one at the top, the parties become stronger together than they were apart. By letting go of "I'm right" and focusing on "We're right," we still meet in the middle, but it's a higher middle that Buddhists call THE WAY.

These triangle templates clearly show that in any relationship, if each of the two parties gives only 50 percent, it is literally impossible for them to connect at a higher level. However, when each party gives 100 percent to the relationship, they connect at the highest physical, mental, emotional, and spiritual points possible, where they become more of who they already are and can accomplish more together than apart.

Do you tend to compromise in your daily work or in your relationships at home? Have you watered down the principles to which you claim to subscribe? Looking hard at the way you resolve conflict with others, are you simply pursuing self-interest and protecting your turf, or do you go the extra mile to create an entirely new, elevated reality with your partner in conflict?

Let us never confuse a win-win situation with a compromised lose-lose situation, where our desire to stay together in business is motivated only by money, or where we stay in an abusive marriage only for the sake of the children.

CHAPTER TWELVE

THE FIVE GAME CHANGERS THAT MAKE 'I' PLAYERS DIFFERENT

Whenever my friends and I show up on a Saturday morning for a pickup basketball game, I am immediately reminded of the difference between a professional world champion 'I' Player athlete committed to a long-term, maximum-performance career, and an amateur, average wannabe focused only on getting by in a short-term, minimum-requirement job.

Because of where we play these games, there are always professional athletes who, during their off season, show up for some competitive exercise. As each game progresses, five game-changing truths make these superstars stand out. They:

- Have a special sense of self
- Think differently
- Prepare differently
- Make everybody around them better
- Rise to the occasion when the game is on the line

A SPECIAL SENSE OF SELF

Having a special sense of self is about knowing who you really are and that we human beings naturally and instinctively fight to survive, not to succumb. The human spirit is the most powerful force in the universe and is controlled by our inherent ability to face our fears and struggle, if necessary, to make it through life's storms. For this reason, our personal value and self-worth should always be the sum total of our thoughts, not the result of a miscalculation and multiplying of our insecurities."

The story is told that when King Louis XVI of France was forced from his throne and imprisoned, his young son, the prince, was taken by those who dethroned the king. They thought that if they could morally destroy the king's son, inasmuch as he was heir to the throne, he would never realize the great and grand destiny that life had bestowed upon him. They took the prince to a community far away, where they exposed the lad to every filthy and vile thing life could offer. They exposed him to foods that would quickly make him a slave to appetite; they constantly used vulgar language around him; they surrounded him with lewd and lustful women; they exposed him to dishonor and distrust. He was surrounded twenty-four hours a day by everything that could drag the soul of a man as low as he could slip.

The prince faced this treatment for more than six months, but not once did he buckle under pressure. Finally, the men questioned him. Why had he not submitted himself to these things. Why had he not partaken? These things—there for the asking—were desirable and would provide pleasure and satisfy his lusts. With a special sense of self, the boy humbly answered, "I cannot do what you ask, for I was born to be a king."

Behavioral scientists, psychologists, and social anthropologists who study human interaction teach that our sense of self affects our relationships more than anything else.

It determines if we can effectively lead, for it is this quality that attracts others to follow us.

How would you evaluate your sense of self, commonly called your self-esteem? Do you know that you are okay just the way you are? If not, why not? How would others rate your self-esteem? What is your greatest quality, character trait, or attribute? Are you physically strong? Are you mentally awake? Are you ethically straight? Do you trust yourself—obey your conscience and follow your gut instincts and promptings? Do others trust you? Is your word and a handshake as good as a legally binding written contract?

Do you have a good sense of humor?
Can you and do you laugh at yourself?

(My dear friend, colleague, and country comedian T. Bubba Bechtol is six feet tall and weighs more than 300 pounds. At the beginning of his comedy show, he always states, "I beat anorexia and I've got it in permanent remission—it isn't coming back!" He says, "I haven't always been this big. I went to the doctor and he put me on a dehydrated food diet for six months. Then one day I got caught in the rain! I gained 150 pounds in five minutes! It was awful!" When Bubba developed chest pains, thank heavens the doctor had a sense of humor too. Bubba explained, "Cut me some slack, Doc—my weight is a medical problem." To which the doctor explained, "No. The only medical problem you suffer from is that your body retains too much chocolate fudge cake!" Bubba countered, "Seriously, Doc, obesity runs in my family." The doctor replied, "No. No one runs in your family!")

Only when you see your self as you really are, why you are, and where you are in your current reality can you change why you are and improve where you are.

THINK DIFFERENTLY

Thinking differently is about answering why you are where you are, why you are doing what you are doing, why you should give it everything you've got when less would be sufficient, and why you should think positive in each and every moment.

For example, a famous shoe manufacturer in England sent two sales representatives to Africa to see if there might be an opportunity to open up a new market and sell more shoes. Both reps returned to London and reported. The first sales professional said, "Nobody in Africa wears shoes. So, there is no market for our products there." The second sales professional reported, "Nobody in Africa wears shoes. So, there's a huge opportunity to open up a new market for our products in Africa!"

Do you see things as they are in terms of biology and probability, or for what they have the power and potential to become in terms of psychology and possibility? Why? Why Not? Do you usually first find the positive in a situation, or do you usually first notice the negative in a situation? Why? Why Not?

When it comes to Thinking Differently, ask yourself and your colleagues:

T is it True?

H is it Helpful?

I is it Inspiring?

N is it a New perspective and disruptive of the old?

K is it Kind?

I is it Important?

N is it Necessary?

G is it really Going to make a significant difference?

Thinking differently is obviously interdependently connected to developing confidence, which sustains your Special Sense of Self, which in turn gives you the deep desire and personal motivation required to Prepare Differently.

PREPARE DIFFERENTLY

Preparing differently is realizing that everybody wants to win, but few are willing to prepare to win. Consequently, you know that the value of something is determined by what you are willing to give up in order to get it. That means what you are doing in any given moment is a conscious choice because you have exchanged precious time of your life that you will never get back. Every conversation, every workday, every practice, and every game really does matter and most definitely deserves your relentless determination and undivided attention so you can perform to the very best of your ability.

Preparing differently had obviously given the world-class athletes mentioned above a competitive advantage in every game. In a professional sense, how many of us act like a Saturday athlete who thinks he can just show up to a sales call; just show up to answer a barrage of irate, unsatisfied customers ranting on call center phone lines; or just show up to efficiently and effectively lead or manage the team?

If we haven't researched the pressing issues of the day and prepared ourselves in every possible way (physically, mentally, emotionally, and spiritually), we can't make the right game-time decisions when they present themselves.

Clearly it was their preparation that allowed these professional athletes to have enough energy at the end of the game to get their bodies to do what their minds wanted them to do—and what their hearts needed them to do. Legendary college football coach Bear Bryant said, "If one of my players is going to quit and give up on himself and his teammates, he is going to quit in practice, not during a game. That's why I make practice so hard!"

How would you evaluate your willingness to Prepare Differently? Are you committed to being a lifelong learner? Why? Why Not? Do you usually compete against others, or do you compete against yourself to make sure you are better today than you were yesterday? Why? Why Not? Are you currently enrolled in a course at a junior college, technical institute, university, or online to increase your knowledge and improve your technical expertise in your job and vocation? Why? Why Not?

MAKE EVERYBODY AROUND YOU BETTER

Making everybody around you better begins when you start treating others as you want to be treated. For example, a prominent local businessman frequently brought his clients to a posh hotel to hold lunch meetings in the lobby restaurant. One day he showed up with his young son. When the boy excused himself to go to the washroom, the general manager asked the father what the special occasion was. The father sadly reported that his son had been diagnosed with cancer and that the next morning he would start his brutal chemotherapy treatments.

Father and son were spending the night, and after their dinner, a dip in the pool, and a movie, the son was going to shave his head to prepare for the morning ordeal. Dad said his son knew he was going to lose his hair anyway and thought that by shaving it, he would be taking a more positive, proactive approach to fighting his cancer and controlling it instead of letting it control him. Dad explained that he too was going to shave his head in a sign of unconditional loving solidarity. The father then asked the manager for a special favor, requesting that when they appeared the following morning for breakfast, the wait staff not react openly to their shaved heads or inquire about the reason they were both bald for fear of embarrassing his son at what was to be the start of the most challenging period of his life.

When they arrived for breakfast, nobody in the room batted an eyelid or said a word. Four of the waiters, however, had also shaved their heads that night too.

As my basketball game progressed, treating others as you want to be treated and inspiring others to be better was an obvious attribute that each of these professional athletes possessed. Because they had first pushed themselves to reach their own ultimate capacity and potential as mentally tough competitors who Think Differently and physically fit specimens who Prepare Differently, they were in a confident mindset and a mentoring heart-set to turn their attention and efforts to helping others do the same by raising the level of play, not only of their teammates but also of their competitors.

Yes, these elite athletes relaxed their efforts during the first three quarters of the game for the same reason any of us do when we feel obligated to relate to the less talented and dumb down our performance for the unprepared.

But by "playing small," we don't inspire ourselves or anyone else, and our competitors get no satisfaction out of beating us when we are not at our best. For this reason, in the last twelve minutes of the game, these athletes literally tutored my team on what it takes to be a champion so they too could become champions.

In the real world, we see people dragging their dreams down to the level of their income when we should be doing whatever is required to raise our income to the level of our dreams.

Simple, but hard, as the path of least resistance is always the easier way. To illustrate: visualize me (Dan) at six-foot-five, weighing 235 pounds, standing on a four-foot-high stage with another man who is five foot-six, weighing 135 pounds, standing on the floor below him. Obviously it is easier for the smaller man to reach up and pull me down to him than for me to reach down and pull the man up to him.

Are you associating with individuals who are dragging you down physically, mentally, spiritually, and emotionally and keeping you from becoming a champion? Remember, you become the average of the five people you associate with the most, and you are definitely judged by the company you keep.

All athletes know that they usually play to the level of their competition, so when you are at your best (physically, mentally, spiritually, emotionally, socially, financially, and with your family), you inspire others to be at their best. To have a best friend, you must first be a best friend, and a best friend is someone who brings out the best in you!

Making others better boils down to treating them as you want to be treated. For example, two men buy identical automobiles that are the same color, with the exact same luxury features and performance options, for the exact same price, on the exact same day. Three years later both men decide to sell their cars on the same day. Are the automobiles still worth exactly the same? If not, why not?

Obviously the value of each vehicle is different, determined solely by how it was treated and cared for. Remember, in sports, in business, in education, in the military, and in everyday life, the goal is to have everybody depart you saying, "I perform at my best when I'm with you—teaching, learning, leading, following, practicing and playing with you, and even competing against you—and will jump at the chance to do it again and again."

Because these professional athletes were truly committed to Making Everybody Around Them Better, at the end of the game they invited everybody on my team to show up at their gym during the week to start working out with them to get in better shape so their games on Saturday mornings would be more competitive.

Because the purpose of a leader is to grow more leaders, who in your organization will you invite into your circle of influence to start mentoring so others can improve themselves and increase their productivity and performance?

RISE TO THE OCCASION

Rising to the occasion when the game is on the line was automatic for these elite athletes because they knew the difference between training to play and training to win, so they refused to lose. In the corporate world you gain a competitive advantage as an individual and grow your market share as an organization, not by doing more than your competition but by doing what your competition is not willing to do.

What most individuals (your competition) are doing is focusing on acquiring knowledge and advanced college degrees and becoming "book smart." What most companies are doing is overinvesting in education, proudly proclaiming they are "learning organizations" and dramatically underinvesting in training.

While other smart and talented individuals and successful organizations are finding it difficult and challenging to innovate and adapt under pressure because they are overeducated and undertrained, valuing knowledge over skill, you will gain and sustain a competitive advantage as an individual because you are "street savvy," and your organization will create and maintain a competitive advantage because it is willing to invest in continuous training to improve the skill level at every pay grade.

This means that under pressure, you will rise to the occasion because the level of your training is higher than most.

This truth about training manifested itself in this basketball game when winning was finally on the line. For the first three quarters of the game (thirty-six minutes), my team had managed to stay ahead of the other team by ten points. But when the final quarter began, something happened.

As if someone turned on a magic hustle/extra effort/high-performance faucet, every time my team got the ball, one of the professional players would come out of nowhere and steal it. He then would pass it to who ever was open to take the shot.

And it didn't matter who made the basket, for he was focused on winning the game—not for his own personal glory but for his teammates because winning was the common goal they all shared and the reason they got together in the first place!

If it were just about exercise, my friends and I could have taken down the hoops and just run, and these superstars would have had no reason to dig deep and step it up to succeed. When there was a play to be made, these guys would make it.

Because of their Special Sense of Self, the way they thought, coupled with their training and incredibly intense preparation, and the personal commitment to make everybody around them better, each professional athlete had the memory of having stepped it up in the past not only to want the ball at crunch time but also to execute and perform in order to make things happen and get the job done when it mattered most.

Will you want the ball at crunch time when your competitor just had a meeting with your potential customer right before your appointment began? Will you handle the pressure to perform and close the sale when it's the end of the quarter and you are below quota, behind the company goal, and there's too much month at the end of your money? As a leader or manager, will you want the tough assignments and difficult negotiations with labor or customers?

Are you willing to do what others in your organization are not willing to do to prepare yourself with extraordinary product knowledge and conscientious work ethic to constantly create high leverage activities and a personal commitment to be better today than you were yesterday? If you are an airman, soldier, marine, or sailor, will you volunteer for the tough, dangerous missions and return with honor? If so, you too will be a champion—world class in both your personal and professional life. You too will turn your success into significance.

How would you evaluate your ability to Rise to the Occasion? Are you willing to come into work early and stay late if required to finish the time-sensitive task at hand without demanding overtime pay? At the end of the day, would your teammates and coworkers actually choose you to be on their team? If you are serving in a military uniform, when it's time to go into battle and it truly is a life -and-death situation, will your brothers in arms trust you enough to choose you to fight beside them?

Gen. Douglas MacArthur said, "On the fields of friendly strife are sown the seeds that on other days and other fields will bear the fruits of victory." Doesn't this sound like Have a Special Sense of Self, Think Differently, Prepare Differently, and Make Everybody around You Better, so you can Rise to the Occasion?

William Arthur Ward wrote: "Do more than belong: participate; do more than care: help; do more than believe: practice; do more than be fair: be kind; do more than forgive: forget; do more than dream: work."

CHAPTER THIRTEEN

THE FIVE STAGES OF A HIGH PERFORMING TEAM

"Teamwork is the complete conviction that nobody
can get there unless everybody gets there."

Once you work on becoming a complete "I" Player, committing to live all Ten "Cs" with no compromise, and are actively attracting other "I" Players to team up with you, the actual process for building a winning team is consolidated into a five-step formula:

INCLUSION

Defined as: "The act of inviting someone to join a club or team, and including that person as part of something larger than themselves. In building a winning team, Inclusion occurs when the group gathers together for the first time to get to know one another, exchange some person information, and make new friends. In this first stage everyone tends to behave quite independently, driven by a desire to be accepted by the others. As you are gathering information and impressions about each other, and about the scope of the task and how to approach it, serious conflicting issues and feelings are avoided, which means not much actually gets done.

REVOLUTION

Defined as: "The forcible overthrow of a social order in favor of a new system." In building a winning team, Revolution occurs when enough initial trust has been developed between individuals that everybody feels safe enough to contribute their ideas, opinions, and experience with confidence and comfortable enough to express discontent and challenge others' opinions. Because they are still a group and not yet a team, tolerance of each other and their differences should be emphasized, and it should be pointed out that disagreements within the group can make members stronger, more versatile, and able to eventually work more effectively as a team, while failure to do so will lower motivation if allowed to get out of control.

RESOLUTION

Defined as: "The action of solving a problem, dispute, or contentious matter." In building a winning team, Resolution is stage three when your group morphs the tolerance of individual differences into the full acceptance of strength in diversity. It is where you proactively decide on one mutually agreed-upon meaningful desired result, and design a plan for the project, requiring everybody to relinquish opinions based on "who is right" and proactively encourage "what is right" to emerge with full agreement with others to make the group function as one.

EVOLUTION

Defined as: "The gradual development of something, especially from a simple to a more complex form." In building a winning team, Evolution is the fourth stage of the process when the group transforms from "me" to "we" and from group to "team" because each member takes individual responsibility to work for both the short-term success and long-term significance of the team's unified goals, knowing they are stronger and better together than they were apart.

EXECUTION

Defined as: "Carrying out or putting into effect a plan, order, or course of action with precision efficiency, mistake-free accuracy, and extraordinary effectiveness." In building a winning team, Execution is the fourth and final stage revealed in three simultaneous events:

At least one person on the team surfaces with the knowledge, technical skills, and competence required to perform each and every task in order to help the team accomplish the collective final desired result.

You and each of your teammates is confident enough to be able to handle the decision-making process without supervision and to find ways to get the job done smoothly and effectively without inappropriate conflict.

One empowered individual rises above the rest as the natural leader (team captain), with no title required, who can and will motivate the others and bind the group together.

Experience reveals that sometimes teams will revert back to the Revolution and Resolution stages when they are required to respond to a change in leadership that challenges the existing norms and dynamics of the team. No worries! Simply engage again in the honest communication that first brought you to your current level of team togetherness, and you will again build a high performing winning team.

"You Can If You Think You Can"

In December 1982, my dear friend Bob Coyne of Brantford, Ontario, decided to host a junior hockey team from Sweden. In exchange, the members of Bob's Canadian junior team would travel to Sweden the following year as guests of the Swedish team. The team from Sweden arrived in Canada on Boxing Day (December 26).

This team was the pride and joy of Stockholm consisting of fourteen and fifteen-year-old boys handpicked from Stockholm and reputed to be a notoriously tough hockey club. As hosts, Bob and his team were to provide the Swedish team with a tour of each of the seven different communities where it would play its seven exhibition games. The final game was to be between the Stockholm team and Bob's Brantford team.

Upon arriving in Canada, the Stockholm team's hope, of course, was to win all seven games and return home with grand tales of victory. It was the first time away from home for these kids. They were suffering from jet lag, and they lost their first game by a dismal 8–1 score. It was a staggering defeat for them. They were a little more prepared for the second game, but again they lost, this time 4–2. They lost the third and fourth games as well. The fifth game was a devastating 9–1 lashing.

At this point in the tour, which was somewhere around New Year's Day, Bob decided they needed a break in the action, a diversion to rally their confidence and rebuild their self-esteem. He arranged a visit to Toronto to see the CN Tower, the National Hockey League Hall of Fame, and other points of interest. The Swedish team would play no hockey for two entire days, but could swim and play basketball at a local high school for entertainment and exercise.

At the end of the Toronto trip, Bob took them to the student center to sit and relax while they waited for the bus to pick them up and take them back to their sponsoring homes. The coach of the Stockholm team asked Bob if there was something he could say to his team that might psych them up for the next game.

Emotional Connection

Bob was neither prepared nor thinking in those terms, but he decided, on the spur of the moment, to see if he could touch their emotions. Bob started talking to them about home, which got them right up off their chairs. He asked them if they missed their moms and dads and if the time change was bothering them. Bob explained that in Stockholm, there were fewer daylight hours during the winter than there were in Canada, and surely this change was affecting them. Bob finally steered the conversation toward hockey, reflecting on their five losses in a row, which surely was not typical of the team, and how they all must feel about these losses. Bob concluded by suggesting that what they needed was something to which they could reach out and relate. He told them that all they needed was the confidence to believe in themselves again. So he left them with a phrase he had heard many other times: "You can if you think you can."

Bob then repeated this phrase to each kid individually while he looked each one squarely in the eye. When he had repeated the phrase to each one of them, he left the room. A few moments later, the bus arrived and they all left. Bob really didn't think he had convinced them, but he went home prepared to reinforce the idea anyway. He made a big sign bearing the phrase YOU CAN IF YOU THINK YOU CAN and took it with him to the next game, which was held at the Six Nations Indian Reservation just south of Francis. Six Nations had a top-notch hockey club, and the Stockholm team knew it. Even prior to arriving in Canada, the Stockholm team was prepared that if it lost a game, it would be either to Six Nations or to Brantford.

Game time arrived, and the Swedish team was still in the locker room. They didn't appear to be coming out, so Bob went in to see what was happening. Most of the team members hung their heads while their coach addressed them, and Bob could see they just weren't up for the game. They turned to look at Bob when he barged in. He smiled broadly and said, "Remember, you can if you think you can!" He waved to the Swedish coach and swiftly exited the locker room.

Hanging The Sign

Bob then hung the sign he had made, unbeknownst to the Swedish team, on the back of their team bench. A minute later, the Swedish team emerged and saw the sign. Spontaneously, every member of the team touched the sign. From there, they went out onto the ice, warmed up, and then faced off to open the game.

Very early on, they took a 1–0 lead, and again they all jumped the boards, touched the sign, and went back out for the face-off. The game continued. The Swedish team scored another goal and again, each member of the team touched the sign. Six Nations came back to tie the game, but for those kids who hadn't won a single game during their entire tour, the tie was as good as a win. The tie put them on top of the world. The noise during the bus ride home was unbelievable!

That brings us to the last day of the tournament. Bob's Brantford team was the Stockholm team's last opponent. He had arranged to pick up the Stockholm team's coach at his hotel room for a pregame lunch. When Bob entered the coach's room, he saw the YOU CAN IF YOU THINK YOU CAN sign propped up on the headboard of the bed. Bob thought it was kind of funny, but he could see that the Stockholm coach really believed it because, as they left for the arena, he grabbed the sign to hang over the bench.

When the Swedish team came onto the ice, they performed the same ritual as they had at Six Nations, each player touched the sign before the start of the game. This final game of the series was a highly competitive, spirited contest and Stockholm beat Brantford by two points. Every time the Swedish team scored, they touched the sign and also skated past Bob's bench grinning and triumphantly shaking their fists at him. There was a party for the team after the game ended, and the next morning, the players flew home to Stockholm.

Going To Sweden

The following December, Bob's team arrived in Stockholm for the exchange tournament. The setup for sports in Sweden is different from the setup in Canada. The Swedes have sports clubs for almost every sport, but all the clubs play in the same arena. The sports building is in downtown Stockholm, and Bob and his junior team went there for a reception following their arrival in Sweden. As they entered the main lobby of the huge, city-owned, government-operated arena, Bob noticed the YOU

CAN IF YOU THINK YOU CAN sign hanging on the wall about twelve feet from the floor. The sign was framed, and beneath it was an inscription of the story of its origin and impact. Bob was surprised, happy, and choked up all at the same time. To this day, that sign still graces the lobby of the Stockholm sports complex, teaching the value of the power of positive thinking to all who enter!

CHAPTER FOURTEEN

DAN CLARK'S 8 STEP FORMULA FOR CREATING A CULTURE OF EXCELLENCE

"Once we get the culture right, the rest of the stuff takes care of itself."—Peter Drucker

How would you describe your organizational culture? Does everybody feel valued and needed? When your employees are asked what they do, do they describe the task they perform everyday - or do they energetically describe the purpose of the greater enterprise?

In our millennial 'gig economy' where employees stay in a job for an average of two years, the focus can't just be on attracting and recruiting top talent. We must focus on retaining our best people through personal development programs they won't get from another employer. The purpose of a leader is to grow more leaders, not generate more followers.

Investing in self-mastery leadership training at every level of your organization will strengthen trust, increase productivity, and create sustained loyalty to your 'value proposition' and to each other!

1. Leaders must present an inspiring and compelling vision of where the team is headed.

2. Leaders and team members must share a passionate purpose with a clear understanding of why the team exists – otherwise it's just a group collection of egos.

3. Leaders (coaches) and team members must create a 'culture of excellence' based on Dan's Ten Commitment 'Cs' to Building A Winning Team, realizing you don't consistently win with the best players – you win with the right people! Honestly evaluate if you can win with the current employees (players) you have on your team. Why or why not?

4. The Leadership team must extend this 'culture of excellence' to include a set of clearly defined "core values" from which you recruit, hire, reward and fire.

5. The leaders and team members must embody the agreed upon "core values" and 'Model' this culture in every way. Remember, people don't do what we say – they do what we do. People join teams and leave jerks!

6. Leaders must attract and recruit "complimentary" types of people – extroverts and introverts – executors and evaluators. If you assemble a team of people that is only like you, it makes your type right and everybody else wrong!

7. Everybody on the team must lead and follow on the same day, encouraging and expecting continuous authentic "feedback" at every level.

8. Leaders and team members must expect and encourage honest celebration for personal victories and organizational 'wins,' which includes acknowledging genuine 'mourning' when

someone leaves the 'tribe,' and finding time outside of work to support one another, which creates and strengthens trust, camaraderie, real friendship, and mutual respect and support inside of work. Because of its importance, take a pause for a moment and think of an 'off work' activity you could help organize and manage that would be exciting and enticing enough to attract your fellow coworkers, team members and leaders to attend that will offer safe and wonderful opportunities to create real friendships and nurture relationship development?

CHAPTER FIFTEEN

THE MAKING OF AN "I" COACH

A championship winning Coach cannot possibly attract "I" players if he/she is not an "I" human being! In a study of the Law of Attraction it is clear that we don't attract who we want – we attract who we are! We attract what we believe we deserve! If we expect someone else to live by the Ten Commitment C's, the only way they will ever respond to our encouragement is if we too, are "I" people. People do what people see, not what people say. "I'd rather see a sermon preached than hear one any day – I'd rather you would walk with me than merely point the way!"

'I' COACHES ARE CRITICAL

From an employee's/player's perspective, unless the coaches, managers, and leaders of the winning team are also "I" people, the team may win short-term, but the organization will never turn into a dynasty.

Coaches and leaders/managers/employers are an integral part of the ecosystem. Do you know that 1% of the earth's surface affects the other 99% and all of humanity's ability to survive? For this reason, I flagged down one of my all-time favorite and most successful coaches to help us dissect the little things that make the big difference. Winning "I" players and championship "I" coaches all "sweat the small stuff."

When I asked him if there is a specific list of ingredients and an accompanying recipe similar to the Ten Cs of being an "I" player that apply especially to coaches (in every field, including teaching, parenting, and managing or leading a corporation), Coach John Pease told me:

"Absolutely! And of all the sports to choose from, I chose to play and coach football for a reason. Football is primal and is the only sport that gets us in touch with our most raw, natural instincts. Unlike basketball and baseball, where you can be cool and chill out, in football you get the crap beat out of you for sixty minutes and with your nose broken, your finger ligaments torn, and your leg muscles pulled, you're forced to do whatever is necessary to survive.

Football requires a mind-set different from anything else because you are hitting and hurting another human being while he hits and hurts you, continually evaluating the difference between pain and injury, and focused 100 percent on overcoming obstacle after obstacle so you don't let anyone else on your team down."

THE CONSUMMATE COACH'S COACH

Coach John Pease is a special man. But what makes him great is not solely his football knowledge. If you coach football, it is a given that you can execute Xs and Os. What makes Coach Pease so extraordinary, and has allowed him to move from good to great to best, and ultimately into being the right coach for each of his teams, is his unwavering belief that any team can win if players simply think and act a certain way.

At the age of twenty-one, Pease began his career coaching eight-man football in Puerto Rico, and for the twenty-five years since then, he has never been on the staff of a losing program. John coached at Long Beach State, the University of Utah (as my coach), and the University of Washington (where they won PAC 10 championships and the Rose Bowl). Coach Pease went on to the pros for three years in the USFL with the Philadelphia Stars, which played in the USFL championship game three years in a row, winning it once. Then he coached four years with the NFL Jacksonville Jaguars, which, in only their second season as a brand-new expansion team, they played in the AFC championship game. Finally, Coach Pease spent nine years with the NFL's New Orleans Saints, which went from thirty-second to fourteenth in the league in just their second season and had their first winning seasons in the history of the team's franchise, which eventually led to a Super Bowl victory in 2010.

TURNING A LOSING PROGRAM AROUND

According to Coach Pease, five things are critical to turning things around in a losing program or a struggling company, and to be an "I" coach, all five are controlled and must be implemented by the coaches/leaders/managers:

A Winning Culture

Create a winning culture, where winning is not only possible, but probable, and, in a short amount of time, expected. Everybody from the top down to the bottom up and all the way sideways must buy into this "possibility thinking." No, it doesn't have to take time. It can be immediate as long as everybody sees and feels that things are not just going to be business as usual. We all know the popular sayings, "If you keep doing what you did, you'll keep getting what you got" and "The definition of insanity is doing the same thing over and over, expecting different results." They especially apply here.

Discipline

Coach Bill Parcells has built winning teams and championship dynasties everywhere he has coached. He took the New York Giants all the way to the Super Bowl. When he took over as head coach of the struggling, losing Dallas Cowboys, the first thing he did was raise expectations both on and off the field. As you recall when some of the veteran players were interviewed on TV during Parcells' first Cowboy training camp, they appeared worn out, saying that the camp was the toughest one they had been to in years.

Higher expectations of discipline were printed on posters and displayed all over camp. They reminded everybody that no one is to be late for practice or meetings, and that every player must sign in and out of a certain number of hours of film study, weight room exercise, training room rehab, and preventive chiropractic and massage therapy. A few players complained that they were grown men being treated like children, but Coach Parcells didn't care. And because of this higher level of enforced discipline, everybody on the team and in the entire Cowboy organization immediately bought into the new winning culture: "No matter what our past has been, we have a spotless future; this is definitely not business as usual."

Belief

Believing that you will win is a higher, truer belief than creating a winning culture that you can win. During Coach Pease's first year coaching the Philadelphia Stars in a game against George Allen's Chicago Blitz in 1983, Philly was behind by seventeen points with five minutes left. Philly fumbled on the twenty-yard line, and as the defense took the field, Pease told his middle linebacker John Bunting, who is now head coach at the University of North Carolina, to have some pride and no matter what, not let Chicago score again. Bunting looked Pease in the eye and said, "We're going to win this game."

Now, Coach Pease and the rest of the staff had already surrendered and thrown in the towel. Well, well, well, Chicago fumbled, and Philly picked up the ball and took it in for a touchdown. Now Philly was down by ten points. With four minutes left, they recover their on-side kick. The Stars score again with one minute and thirty seconds to go. Now down by three, they stop Chicago, get the ball, and kick a field goal to tie the game! In overtime, Philly takes the opening kickoff and marches eighty yards without throwing a pass to win the game.

From that day on, Coach Pease has believed and instilled in each of his players on every team to never quit! And because he is an "I" coach, no matter where he goes he always brings and creates great chemistry, making every other coach on the staff better, and makes sure no one ever thinks for even a minute that they cannot win.

Isn't it interesting that the attitudes and commitment to excellence of players, employees, and subordinates to execution can influence the attitudes and commitments of their coaches and employers? In the Philly game, everybody in the organization not only had to come to believe that they could win, but also that they would win – especially the offensive coaches who called the plays in the last 80-yard touchdown drive.

Positive Self-talk

Exemplify and teach positive self-talk. If you go to your computer, get online, and type in "bad football plays," it will spit out maybe 120 articles that have bad football plays in them. And if you put in "good football plays," you will find about 120 articles about good plays. So what is the strongest, most efficient computer in the world? Our minds!

Because you are at the keyboard of your own mind and in total control of input and output, don't put in any bad plays or negative behaviors. Our minds will agree with what we tell them to agree with, and our bodies always follow what our minds say. If you tell yourself that today is going to be an unbearable and miserable day, or that you're going to have a lousy practice, or that you're tired and aren't going to make any more sales calls, then you are absolutely right.

On the flip side, if you enter positive expectations, you will definitely get matching, positive results. This ties directly into Coach John Pease's last point to creating a championship dynasty.

Everybody Matters

Everybody in the organization matters. When Pease coached with Don James at the University of Washington, Coach James demanded that the players on the team who never got into a game be treated like the best players. Even the walk -on players were just as important as the starters. When Washington played in the Sun Bowl, the team was allowed to bring 95 of its 135 players for the week. Three days before the game, the team could fly in the rest of the players to participate in festivities and to be on the sideline.

The Sun Bowl made its customary 110 Sun Bowl watches to present to the players at the opening banquet. Coach James phoned the committee chairman and explained that he had twenty-five other players and needed to buy them Sun Bowl watches as well. The Sun Bowl committee told him that they had destroyed the mold and it was too late to make any more.

Coach James told the committee that he would pay to have a new mold made because he wanted all of his players to get exactly the same thing. The Sun Bowl told him it couldn't do that, and Coach James simply replied, "We're not coming then."

Everyone who knows Don James knows he would not have gone. With time running out, the Sun Bowl committee broke down, and every Washington player got an official Sun Bowl watch. This was a true symbol of what football teaches: all for one and one for all – one heartbeat, one dream.

CHAPTER SIXTEEN

BEING AN "I" COACH

As our time together was winding down, I asked Coach Pease what qualities and traits he looks for in players when building a winning team. Because he was a member of the first staff, and was on the ground floor of creating from scratch a brand new team in the NFL, I knew he could shed some light on this process and even add to our Two "Is" and Ten "Cs."

To set the stage, the Jacksonville Jaguars were an NFL expansion team. To start it up, the NFL conducted what it called a "supplemental draft," with each existing team putting players in a pool that Jacksonville could choose from. To keep the process fair, when Jacksonville took a team's player, that team could then take back a player from the pool. This way a team would not lose too many good players. Jacksonville also got two draft choices per round – a first pick and a last pick. Having "best" players is the secret to great coaching.

Question:

What were you looking for from these best players in the supplemental draft?

JP:

First of all let's clarify they were the best 'available' players. I agree with what you teach about great or best companies and great or best people only being relevant and dependent on what you compare them with. That's why great and best is not good enough. We all know that every structure is only as strong as its foundation.

I agree with your two "Is" and TEN "Cs" but would add, "I am responsible for me." It's Independent Individual Preparation based on individual responsibility. It's about Ten "Bs": Be honest, Be organized, Be smart, Be disciplined, Be respectful, Be on time, Be accountable for your actions, Be curious about your full potential, Be relentless in your work ethic, Be committed to doing what's necessary to succeed.

The head coach of our Jacksonville Jaguars was inherently intense, gruff, and non-complimentary, which came across as negative. Consequently, our players had to finally take ownership of the team by following the Ten "Bs," and no longer wait for the coach to create a positive chemistry and compliment them. They started encouraging and complimenting each other, raising the level of team expectations, policing each other, and looking out for one another's best interests on and off the field.

Soon, they discovered that it was what they did when the coach was not around that made them true champions, and come game time, they really weren't doing anything for the coaches. They were giving it everything they had for each other and themselves!

Question:

You mentioned that when you were in the army, you coached eight-man football on post in Puerto Rico. Is what you are explaining here similar to what happens to our men and women in the military when the fighting begins? From what I have heard, it's during combat that our troops connect with each other at the deepest, most emotional trust level.

JP:

Absolutely! I've always made sure that each and every player in my small "position" group (linebackers or defensive linemen) has a soldier mentality. Although he may get wounded, he still must man his machine gun, because if he doesn't continue to cover his platoon's right flank, his fellow soldiers, his fellow teammates, his fellow brothers-in-arms are going to get shot and killed. My guys always know that no one leaves his post, and no one will ever be left behind. There is a huge difference between pain and injury.

Individual 'Position' Identity

On every team I have been affiliated with, I knew that more important than anything else, I had to lead, inspire, and expect every group of players that I coached, regardless of whether they were linemen or linebackers, to be the best, most tight-knit band of brothers on the team. No matter what, my players always took pride in working the hardest and being the toughest, most disciplined, dedicated, and, of course, most emotionally intense, mentally irregular guys on the squad!

It was my job to mold several personalities into one proud identity, where everybody knew, both on and off our team that you mess with one of us, you mess with all of us! We truly were our "brother's keepers." I looked out for each of them, they looked out for each other, and we all looked out for our team of warriors.

Groups of NFL defensive linemen have done this for years, attracting famous nicknames based on their unique reputation as a group. The defensive front of the L.A. Rams were called the "Fearsome Foursome." The four linemen of the Minnesota Vikings were called the "Purple People Eaters." The Pittsburg Steelers defense was known as the "Steel Curtain," and the eleven players on the defensive unit of the undefeated Super Bowl champion Miami Dolphins were collectively called the "No Name Defense."

The overly big, charismatic offensive linemen on the Washington Redskins were affectionately called the "Hogs." Getting my guys to be proud of each other and honored to be identified with their individual group is the one thing that always made me a successful assistant coach and is the key to building an entire winning organization. Your "I" approach to team building is absolutely right on the money as you create a championship dynasty – one player, one practice, one small group, one game at a time!

Pride In Job Description Identity

This applies in the corporate arena on the company team, too. The accounting department, the sales reps, the marketing organization, the national account executives, the support staff, the plant managers and the assembly line supervisors, all have their own unique groups with a potential group personality and known identity.

In education you have the teachers, principals, superintendents, counselors, secretaries, custodians, and librarians all playing their own unique position. In the Air Force you have the Generals, The Non-Commissioned officers, Wing Commanders, pilots, maintainers, officers and enlisted. Regardless if it's sports, education, business, or military, establishing a group identity allows you to create a healthy, fun inter-departmental competition that will ignite everybody's passion, creativity, and imagination to beat their coworkers.

Coach John Pease is a hero coach to many players, including me. He has left a lasting legacy of leadership and love everywhere he has gone. He proves that winning is easy, winning is contagious, and winning builds on itself. The more you win, the more players start taking ownership of the team and pride in their performance both on and off the field.

Coach Pease also proves that of the "TEN Cs" required to build a winning team, chemistry is the most critical, especially in creating a long-term championship dynasty. It is chemistry that reveals the presence or absence of all the other NINE Cs. Coach Pease is the consummate "I" players' coach because he is the prototype "I" coach! Each of us can and should be, too!

Yes, the ingredients for building a winning team include all we have presented. Coaches (employers) and players (employees) need to inculcate all TEN Cs of the Two "Is" in winning into their everyday thoughts, behaviors, and habits. Coaches should passionately share their expectations and their traditions in order to develop unity and establish continuity between the past, present, and future.

Finally, anyone who is responsible for building any kind of team – at home, school, work or play – must remember that everybody else in their same league, industry and situation is also tasked to build a winning team.

If you are not relentlessly pursuing perfect execution by working and tweaking and pushing yourself to your ultimate capacity and potential as a human being, someone else, somewhere else, is. When you meet him, he will win. Because of the nature of this competition, you are going to win some games and lose some championships; win some sales and lose some business. This is not okay, but it IS why we coach and manage: for the excitement, for the adrenaline rush, for the thrill and challenge of playing a human chess game, and especially for the opportunity to positively touch the lives of others, influence them to succeed, and inspire them to become significant.

If you are not relentlessly pursuing perfect execution by working and tweaking and pushing yourself to your ultimate capacity and potential as a human being, someone else, somewhere else, is. When you meet him, he will win. Because of the nature of this competition, you are going to win some games and lose some championships; win some sales and lose some business. This is not okay, but it IS why we coach and manage: for the excitement, for the adrenaline rush, for the thrill and challenge of playing a human chess game, and especially for the opportunity to positively touch the lives of others, influence them to succeed, and inspire them to become significant.

CHAPTER SEVENTEEN

EVALUATING, RECRUITING & ATTRACTING THE RIGHT TALENT

Every organization and every team share one key commonality: their success is dependent on recruiting top talent. Obviously by now you know the difference between 'recruiting' and 'attracting' – the difference between hiring a 'mercenary hired gun' motivated by fame and fortune, and converting a 'missionary believer' motivated by cause and effect – which manifest themselves in the difference between training to fight, and training to win!

In the world of education, we know you can have an old-fashioned, crumbling, dilapidated, outdated school building in a bad neighborhood, with an amazing and passionate principal administrator, who leads a teaching staff of smart, competent, caring, talented, passionate educators, and still give the students whom they serve a tremendous quality education.

The football team at Kahuku High School in Hawaii play on the worst field – a hard dirt field with no grass and poor facilities, and yet year in and year out they are ranked in the top ten high school football programs in the country (many times the #1 team in America) because of their incredible, competent and passionate coaches who get their players to buy into the system they run.

And… you can have a brand new, state of the art, beautiful school building and a new all turf football stadium with amazing locker room facilities, and yet because the Principal administrator is incompetent and the classroom teachers are just going through the motions (confusing teaching with talking), and the football coaches have a mediocre system that doesn't inspire any athletes to give it their 'all,' the students perform poorly on the standardized tests and the team loses every game. Why?

It's not about identifying and hiring the 'best' principal and the best coach. It's about attracting the 'right' person to lead the school, the right in-class room educators to teach the students, and attracting the right person to be the head coach.

Leaders of great companies ask: First Who, Then What? If your company's at a standstill, you may be asking the wrong question.

In his book, Good To Great, author Jim Collins creates a lasting and memorable metaphor by comparing a business to a bus and the leader as a bus driver. He emphasizes that it is crucial to continuously ask "First Who, Then What?"

You are a bus driver. The bus, your company, your school, your athletic team, your military Group/Wing/Battalion/Squadron/ Platoon is stuck, stagnant, at a standstill, and it's your job to get it going. You have to decide where you're going, how you're going to get there, and who's going with you. Most people assume that great bus drivers immediately start the journey by announcing to the people on the bus where they're going – by setting a new direction or by articulating a fresh corporate/team/military unit vision.

However, the real starting point and most significant and long lasting decision of the bus driver/leader/coach is not to begin with 'where' but with 'who.' In fact, whenever you're confronted with any problem or opportunity, it is critical that you shift the decision from a question of 'what should we do?' into a decision of 'who would be the right person to take responsibility for this?' This means that when we are building any kind of a winning team, we must spend a significant portion of time on people decisions: get the right people on the bus, get the right people in the right seats, get the wrong people off the bus, and develop the right people into bigger seats for your 'succession plan.'

For this reason, extraordinary 'significant' leaders/coaches have taken the time to develop a disciplined, systematic process for getting the right people on the bus, and they stick with that discipline – first the people, then the direction – no matter what happens or why and how and when the circumstances change.

Again, it's first 'who' – the unique ones who have already identified their personal 'why,' then 'what,' 'how' and 'when.' This is a simple straightforward four step process:

COLLIN'S BUS ANALOGY

1. Make Sure The Bus Is Ready To Drive

Let's face it. Sometimes we are hired to drive a broken bus. And yes, we first must fix what's broken. The good news is that most of the time the bus (organization) doesn't need a complete overhaul. The engine is working fine and the tires and body and seats are in perfect working order. All that is wrong is that the brakes are stuck and there is no gas in the tank. The fuel gauge is on empty and the brake lights are on! In this metaphor, what constitutes the gas and why is the tank empty?

It's not empty. It's just full of the wrong fuel that cannot fire up the engine! It's full of 'mission' instead of 'purpose.'

For example, the Disney Institute is known for its relentless focus on purpose in getting everyone they hire to work at Disneyland and Disneyworld to share in an intangible dream, and not just work for a paycheck. Disney's published purpose is: "To create happiness for others." Which means that it doesn't matter if an executive is in an office leading people/managing operations, or if an employee parks cars, cleans up the property, sweeps the grounds, works graveyard, operates a ride, maintains the facilities, acts in costume as a Disney character, or sells merchandise in a store, whatever they do is contributing to 'creating happiness for others.'

My friend and colleague Simon Sinek, author of Start with Why, explains why this concept is so important for every organization in every industry today: "Studies show that over 80 percent of Americans do not have their dream job. If more knew how to build organizations that inspire, we could live in a world in which that statistic was the reverse – a world in which over 80 percent of people loved their jobs. People who love going to work are more productive and more creative. They go home happier and have happier families. They treat their colleagues and clients and customers better. Inspired employees make for stronger companies and stronger economies."

When you combine the example of Disney's purpose with the wisdom of Sinek, it is clear that when you convert your organizational mission statement into a purpose statement, the leaders of your organization can expect everybody to choose to obey.

Mission – What To Do – Why You Do It

- Mission Focuses on Operating a Business; Purpose Focuses on Sharing a Dream
- A Mission is Strategic; Purpose is Cultural
- A Mission is Motivational; Purpose is Aspirational
- A Mission Creates "Buy-In"; Purpose Instills "Ownership"
- A Mission Provides Focus; Purpose Fuels Passion
- A Mission Builds a Company; Purpose Builds a Community
- A Mission Lays Bricks; Purpose Builds Cathedrals
- A Mission Parks Cars; Purpose Creates Happiness

2. Get The Right People On The Bus

Leaders/coaches must religiously teach and exemplify and expect each of the employees/players/educator's/military personnel to be anxiously engaged in becoming 'I' Players by subscribing to and living by the Ten 'C' Commitments of Clarity, Character, Competence, Consistency, Competitiveness, Cause, Chemistry, Contribution, Cohesion, and Conclusion. The competitive advantage comes when you invest substantial time in evaluating each candidate and make systematic use of the five evaluation techniques: Telephone and personal Interviews, Character References, Background Checks, Personality Tests, and my favorite: Observation. That's right. Proof?

My wife and I have been to the Kentucky Derby many times. We have always gone with a very wealthy, influential group of sophisticated horse owners and racing fans who love to gamble and bet big bucks on their favorite stallions. Consequently, when we arrive in our VIP tent and start to eat and drink, the big shots pull out their papers that detail the 'handicaps' of each race, and start explaining to our group the pedigree of each horse, which supposedly dictates whether they are fast on dirt or turf, and who should win the fast pace sprint part of the race and which horse is best in the longer distances. It's all listed in their special addition newspapers published at Churchill Downs and other places especially for Derby Day.

The most amusing part of each of the Kentucky Derby race days is the fact that regardless of what the handicap info papers said, my wife picked the winning horse in most of the nine races that day and ALWAYS picked the Kentucky Derby Winner that won the roses! Frustrated, each of these big time horsemen gamblers wanted to know how my wife picked the horse. Her answer is most revealing when nit comes to the 'observation' of talent and evaluating winners. When the horses were brought out to the 'Paddock' and paraded around in front of the crown before each race, my wife picked out the cockiest, most confident, strutting stallion in the field and bet her money where her eyes and gut were! Reluctantly, I never followed her advice and still only bet a hundred bucks on her recommendation. But... by the middle of race day, everybody in our group had thrown their official papers away and were simply asking, "Okay, which horse is the biggest stud? Which one is going to win?"

When in doubt, do not bring the person on the bus. Let a seat go unfilled – until you have found the right person. Ensure your company/ team/military unit does an exceptional job of retaining the right people on the bus to perpetuate your good hiring decisions for a very long time.

- The right people have personal values that closely align with a company's core values. They can articulate these values and are willing to promote and spread them to others.
- The right people do not have to be tightly managed. They expect delegation, and don't thrive in a control-oriented hierarchy.
- The right people understand they don't have a job; they have a responsibility to achieve results. When you fly, do you want the air traffic controller to have a job directing airplanes, or a responsibility to land planes safely?
- The right people do what they say they will do and want to be held accountable for results. They are careful about what they commit to and deliver 100% on their commitments.
- The right people practice "window/mirror thinking". When things go well they are transparent, pointing out success factors in others and not taking all the glory. When things don't go well, the glass window becomes a mirror they face, and take responsibility.
- The right people have a real passion for the organization and the work it does.

3. Get The Right People In The Right Seats

Have 100% of the key seats on the bus filled with the right people. This doesn't mean 100% of ALL seats have the right people, but 100% of the key seats. If you think there might be a "wrong who," first give the person the benefit of the doubt that perhaps he or she is in the wrong seat. Whenever possible, give a person the chance to prove himself or herself in a different seat, before drawing the conclusion that he or she is a wrong person on the bus.

Spotting The Right Talented Winners
(Excerpts From An Article By Coach Mike Palma)

"Evaluating talent becomes the difference between the winners and the losers. There are two kinds of talent in any field, in my opinion. Let's call them 'Original Talent' and 'Derivative Talent.' The original talent is one-of- a-kind. Their work and skills are special and distinct – nobody does it quite the way they do it. The derivative talent is skilled and able – but replaceable. Gifted – but not indispensable.

I've found that it's difficult to separate the "game" from the recruit. If a kid plays the game "the right way" – he's probably a solid dude. If he is a shuck and 'jiver' on the court – that's probably the way he is off of it. It's a little trickier with what I call 'creatives,' but it's difficult to separate the person from the portfolio. The trick is to discover if the book matches the recruit. So how do you do that? What can you do to more creatively and effectively recruit and evaluate more judiciously?

The Walk

Before I'd watch a recruit play in a game, I just wanted to see how he walked. I could tell a lot by that. So I'd get to the gym early to be there for the JV game so I could watch the kid walk into the gym, and then walk into the locker room to dress out. His posture, balance, gait and grace literally signaled how "grounded" he was. I looked for something I call a "humble swagger." All the great ones have this. Some have more of one than the other. But I look for the perfect balance. I was surprised at first that "The Walk" also applied to creative talent, (a slouch is a slouch). Greatness begins from the ground up, not the neck down.

Good Hands/Firm Handshake

It's amazing how many great athletes can't catch the ball. They can run like a banshee and jump out of the gym but throw some of them a pass from 18 feet with some zip on it and it's concrete city. Coaches that subscribe to "the best available athlete" theory of recruiting often wind up with a team prone to turnovers. Be honest. Have you ever gotten the dead-fish handshake? It was somewhat in vogue about ten years ago. It creeps me out. Or the Fred Flintstone hand shake, where you need to ice down your hand afterwards? In sport and in business, I want people with sure hands and solid handshakes on my team.

Eye Contact

I'm not a shrink but I know poor eye contact signals evasiveness or worse, insincerity. As a coach, I would never recruit a kid who didn't look me in the eye. They didn't have to say a lot, but they had to make consistent eye contact. When I recruit a Creative Director for an agency, I make a point to try to meet him. They've got to look me in the eye when they explain why they are motivated by the opportunity. If not, it's lip service.

See Them Sweat

How are they under adversity? Do they exhibit grace under pressure? Do they handle victory and defeat with equal dignity?

These are key indicators of character. Are they truly competitive (true competitors need to compete, NOT win)? Truly competitive people never accept in victory what they would not accept in defeat.

For all of these reasons, we need to recruit in person. Yes, in our digital world of the Internet and videos, we should use these resources only as a preliminary capturing inbox and sifting process to get to the finalists. However, the biggest problem with video evaluation of talent is that you never get to see the person/potential employee/player actually sweat. There is no perspiration on video.

This is where online recruiting really hampers small and mid-sized creative agencies. It leaves them more vulnerable than ever to poor fits. It seems easy, post an ad for a job and count the resumes. The problem is, the top talent – the Original Talent – is not looking on web sites for a job. They're playing. And winning. Online recruiting is shallow and sterile. You get a hundred resumes and ninety of them are blatantly poor fits with no agency experience. They get deleted on contact. Ten of them are potential recruits. Of these ten, five are truly interested in the opportunity. Now how do you evaluate those five? They will be pretty adept on the phone, they're ad people – they know how to talk and sell themselves. I prefer to watch them walk, shake their hand, observe a peculiar trait, watch their confident eye contact, and sweat – knowing when you sweat more in peace you will bleed less in war!

4. Get The Wrong People Off The Bus

Ask yourself, "Can I win with the current employees/players/military personnel I have?" If you inherit a group of employees/players who are not committed to learning and perfecting the Ten 'C' Commitments in their lives, the sad and brutal reality is: if you can't change the people, you change the people.

Sometimes you let people go because that one person's particular skill no longer matches up with your newly created or revitalized system (as in a drop back throwing quarterback who in your new system needs to be able to run); or a particular person balks at the new direction you are taking the organization, or complains about the mandatory new training and refuses to re-wire his thinking. This isn't to say he/she is not competent and cannot be an asset to a different organization. It's just that he/she doesn't fit into your particular model of 'bus.' Once you fill your bus with the right people in the right seats, it becomes less a question of where you're headed – and instead, how far you can go.

CHAPTER EIGHTEEN

SIGNIFICANT COACHES MAKE
TEACHING/MENTORING PERSONAL

In my sophomore year of high school, I met an anthropology teacher, Mr. Tom Croft. I was a tall, gangly, insecure kid who only went to class to stay eligible for athletic competition. I didn't know anything about anthropology except that "we came from the goo, went through the zoo, and now we're you, whoop-dee-doo," so I never signed up for Mr. Croft's class. The intriguing thing about this is that it didn't stop him from positively impacting my life.

One day, many years after I graduated, I tracked him down to discuss mutual respect and support in the context of positive discipline. I was looking for a firsthand experience from the world of education that would apply to parenting, coaching, and the corporate world of management, sales, and customer service. The conversation centered on how to motivate, inspire, and empower others – not only to increase performance and productivity, but to keep the rules and show respect.

Mr. Croft asked for my definitions. With regard to mutual respect and support, I said, "The only place from which a person can grow is where he or she is."

For positive discipline, I said, "You cannot increase a person's performance by making him or her feel worse; humiliation immobilizes behavior."

Mr. Croft's eyes lit up with excitement as he shared the following experience to illustrate his point. "I had a student who disrupted everything," he said.

"Did you send him to the office?" I asked.

With an offended look on his face, he said, "I've taught school for more than twenty-five years, and I've never sent a student to the principal." Mr. Croft laughed. "Most of my colleagues think the principal has all the Band-Aids. No way. Teachers are responsible for their classrooms and the development and education of each kid. You don't just throw them out when they do something wrong. We have to invite them to grow. We must catch them doing something right."

"Mr. Croft," I interrupted, "I've been to schools where a long line of students trails out the principal's office, down the hall, out the door, and past the 9A bus stop. They're suntanned! And they just stand there with that look of 'Yep, I screwed a goldfish into the pencil sharpener four months ago, and I'm on *murders row*, still waiting to see the principal.' If this is education, we're fooling ourselves! So what did you do with your student?" I asked.

"Interesting you should ask," he replied. "I didn't give up on him. My research uncovered that this James character played in a rock-and-roll band and that he was playing that Friday night in a smoke-filled, honky-tonk, redneck biker bar out in the bushes somewhere. I talked five teachers into going with me so I wouldn't be stabbed all by myself."

"Then what happened?" I asked expectantly.

"Now picture this," Mr. Croft continued. "Six of us in argyle sweaters with matching socks stood at the back of the dance floor surrounded by teenagers who looked like they'd been mugged with a staple gun. The lead singer had a carburetor stuck in his nose. When James spotted us, he leaned into the microphone and asked, 'What are you proctologist-looking teachers doing here?' We told him we heard his band was awesome and wanted to check them out."

Mr. Croft and his colleagues only stayed fifteen minutes. That's all the noise they could take. That was Friday night. On Monday morning, was James a discipline problem in Mr. Croft's class? No way. Was he a problem in Mr. Croft's class the rest of the school year? No way! Was James a discipline problem in other teachers' classrooms for the rest of the school year? Yes! Was it because they couldn't teach? No. It was simply because they didn't care.

"What Goes Around Always Comes Back Around"

Mr. Croft was a teacher twenty-four hours a day – in the grocery store on Saturday, in the park on Sunday afternoon, after school, before school, and in and out of his classroom. Mr. Croft inspired and taught every student at East High, especially me. He encouraged me to become all I could possibly be. How could I possibly repay Mr. Croft?

A few years after I graduated from high school, I had an opportunity to coach Pop Warner football for thirteen-year-olds who had never played before. To get a feel for the boys' abilities, I lined them up into two rows and had each of them run out for a pass. I wanted to see who could run, catch, and throw so I could formulate a team in my mind.

Two days into practice, a tall, gangly, insecure kid wearing a new shirt, new jeans, and new loafers showed up on the field. I asked him if he didn't want to go home and change his clothes. He boldly replied, "I've already missed two days of practice, and I don't want to miss anymore. I came to play ball!"

He got in line, and when he ran out for a pass, I threw the ball. It hit him square in the head. He picked up the ball and ran it back to me. He slapped it into my chest and ran to the other line. It came time for his second pass and I hit him in the head again. With his nose bleeding and his lip swelling, he picked up the ball, raced it back to me, and got back in line.

On his third attempt, I lofted a soft, easy pass, but it was over his head. He dove for the ball, but came up nowhere near it. Covered with grass stains from head to toe, his body messy, mucky, and soaking wet, he got up, took the muddy ball, raced back to me, and slapped it to my chest. Figuring I'd better have a chat with him before he killed himself, I pulled him out of line and asked, "Why are you here? Does your dad want you to be a football star? Did your friends talk you into it?"

I will never forget the moment he looked up with his big brown eyes and said, "Coach, I'm here because I want to play football. And I promise if you'll help me, I know I can do it!"

"What's your name?" I asked.

He shyly answered, "Tommy Croft."

Shocked, I asked if his dad taught anthropology at East High School. Surprised, he replied, "I think so."

"Get back in line," I told him. Here, at last, was my chance to be a Mr. Croft to a Croft! Here was my chance to give something back. For the first time in my life, I understood the meaning of "an educational system." What goes around really does come back around!

"Take It Personally"

The greatest educator, Horace Mann, was asked to be the guest speaker at a dedication service for a beautiful new high school building. Standing on the stage of a state- of-the-art auditorium, he concluded by gesturing and saying, "All the sacrifice, hard work, time, and money that went into this magnificent edifice will be worth it if we but help one child."

As Mr. Mann was exiting the building, a parent confronted him. "Didn't you overstate it a little, that all this would be worth it if we just help one child?" the parent asked. Horace Mann, in his wisdom, simply replied, "No. What if that child was yours?!"

The next time we complain against tax levies and bond issues to improve our school systems, let us take it personally and vote yes for education!

"Support Always Increases Performance"

John McMaster became a superstar basketball player in high school. For each of his three years on the team, he was All-Conference, and All-State. In his final season, he was named the Most Valuable Player in the league. John's mother never missed a game at home or away, regardless of the travel distance or weather conditions. She always bought a season pass and was always in the bleachers cheering her son to victory. Interestingly, John's mother was totally blind. What's the message? Although the mother could not see her son, he could see her. Support makes the special difference!

"Service Transforms Both The Receiver And The Giver"

A unique directive was initiated at a high school in northern Utah, where students with a physical or mental challenge were fully integrated into the mainstream classes and curriculum. To make it work, the administration organized a mentor program that teamed up one special-needs student with a mainstream student who would help him or her along.

The athletic director presented the idea to the captain of the football team. John was a tall, strong, intense young man — not the patient, caring type needed for this kind of program. He made it clear that this "wasn't his thing" and he didn't have time to be a mentor. But the athletic director knew it would be good for him and insisted that John volunteer.

John was matched up with Randy — a young man with Down syndrome. Reluctant and irritated at first, John literally tried to "lose" Randy, but soon John welcomed the constant company. Randy not only attended every one of John's classes and ate with him at lunch time, he also went to football practice.

After a few days, John asked the coach to make Randy the official manager responsible for the balls, tape, and water bottles. At the end of the football season, the team won the state championship, and John was awarded with a gold medal as the Most Valuable Player in the state. Randy was presented with a school letterman jacket. The team cheered as Randy put it on. It was the coolest thing that had ever happened to him; from that day forward, Randy never took it off. He slept in his jacket and wore it throughout each weekend.

Basketball season started, and John was also the captain and star of that team. At John's request, Randy was again named the manager. During the basketball season, they were still inseparable. Not only did John take Randy to special occasions — like dances as a joint escort for his girlfriend — but he also took Randy to the library to tutor him in his classes. As he tutored Randy, John became a much better student and made the honor roll for the first time in more than a year. The mentor program was unveiling itself as the most rewarding year of John's life.

Then tragedy struck in the middle of the state basketball tournament. Randy caught a virus and suddenly died of pneumonia. The funeral was held the day before the final championship game. John was asked to be one of the speakers. In his talk, John shared his thoughts about his deep, abiding friendship and respect for Randy. He told how Randy had been the one who had taught him about real courage, self-esteem, unconditional love, and the importance of giving 100 percent in everything he did. John dedicated the upcoming state finals game to Randy and concluded his remarks by stating that he was honored to have received the MVP award in football and the Leadership Plaque for being the captain of the basketball team.

"But," John added, "the real leader of both the football and basketball teams was Randy, for he accomplished more with what he had than anyone I've ever met. Randy inspired all who knew him." John walked from behind the podium, took off the irreplaceable, twenty- four-carat-gold state football MVP medallion that hung around his neck, leaned into the open casket, and placed it on Randy's chest. He placed his captain's plaque next to it.

Randy was buried in his letterman jacket, surrounded by John's cherished awards, as well as pictures and letters left by others who admired him. But this is not the end. The next day, John's team won the championship and presented the game ball to Randy's family. John went to college on a full athletic scholarship and graduated with a master's degree in education. Today John is a special education teacher and volunteers ten hours a week for the Special Olympics.

CHAPTER NINETEEN

CREATING A CHAMPIONSHIP DYNASTY

"I see no virtue where I smell no sweat. If you don't invest very much, then defeat doesn't hurt very much, and winning is not very exciting."—NFL Coach Dick Vermeil

Creating a championship dynasty begins with building a winning team filled with "I" players/employees. But in order to take yourself, your business—any organization—and your team to the ultimate level and consistently win, requires a deeper understanding of two of the TEN Cs and a lesson on the making of an "I" coach/leader/ manager. The two Cs that need further emphasis and illustration are clarity of Cause and creating Chemistry.

CLARITY OF CAUSE

Individuals, businesses, organizations of any kind, and teams who execute for one game; or focus for one sales cycle from prospecting to closing the deal; or become profitable immediately after the entrepreneurial enterprise is launched, do so because they have become good or great or even best and well-trained in the peripherals of success: blocking, tackling, throwing, catching, batting, putting, driving, typing, filing, selling, marketing, promotions, quality control and service.

Even in the world of religion we see members of churches going through the peripheral motions of regularly attending mass, church, or synagogue; pay their tithes and offerings; abstain from alcohol, tobacco, drugs, and profanity; eat more grains and natural foods; and even fast once a month. But fasting without a clear purpose and deep understanding of prayer is nothing more than going without food. My point?

Becoming brilliant at the basics is critical to winning. But in order to create a long- lasting world-class business and a championship dynasty in sports, we must know more and do more than the obvious outward peripheral things. To capitalize on our religious example, to keep church members active and involved requires more of them than merely keeping the legalistic traditions.

Clear and concise clarity of Cause constitutes the central doctrine of an organization, and is the catalyst for conversion and conviction of new and existing members. It is often referred to as expectations and vision. High expectations must be set first by ourselves for ourselves and then by someone whom we deeply respect, who will stretch us to perform at a higher level than we would all by ourselves.

When internal and external expectations match, we run when the coach is not around, we work when the employer is not around, we study when the teacher is not around, and we willingly pay the price today so we can enjoy the prize forever—the prize of personal "I" pride achievement, self- actualizing peace and tranquility, and a magnificently rewarding life of significance!

This deeper understanding of vision is not an ordinary interpretation. It is usually inspired by a basic idea that soon transforms itself into an unstoppable power that knows no bounds. Personal vision is internal expectation, but it's the shared vision of external expectation that brings an organization close together, enabling team members to help each other win.

CAN'T BUY CHEMISTRY

Although clarifying the cause, individually and collectively as a team, is the starting place of building a winning team and sustaining a winning streak, without chemistry, nothing of a long -term nature will ever exist or sustain itself. Everybody wants to win and every coach and employer, player and employee, usually shares that vision.

Clarity of cause is easy to fix and inspire. However, we must remember that a lot of teams have a lot of very expensive highly paid "I" players on them who want to win but still don't win. The New York Yankees, the Washington Redskins, and the Los Angeles Lakers have all had at one time the highest salary base in their leagues, and yet they still could not win a championship.

After the so-called U.S. "Dream Team" of the 2004 Summer Olympic Games lost several basketball games in Greece, and in no way even came close to winning the championship, a *USA Today* headline read, "680 Million Dollars Couldn't Buy the USA a Gold Medal!"

So what was lacking? We've already discussed *best* players versus *right* players and that it's easy to erroneously believe that if players have three out of the TEN Cs, you can create a winning team.

Five out of the six individual elements make you a *best* player, and with enough *best* players, the team can win some games. But to sustain a winning streak, and eventually create long-term domination of your opponents, not only do all six of the Independent attributes have to be present in each employee/player, but both Interdependent elements of Contribution (because it's what you do when the coach is not around that matters, you give it everything you've got when less would be sufficient) and Cooperation (it's not who is right but what is right) must be present in *every employee/player as well as in every leader/manager/coach.*

We need both "Is" in winning because they don't give out Super Bowl rings one at a time! Interdependent collaboration, which is a commitment to contribute, participate, serve, and make everybody around us better, is illustrated by the two university teams who have more players playing in the National Football League than any other colleges—Penn State and Notre Dame.

Players at these schools do not have their individual names on the back of their jerseys. Each player realizes and firmly believes that the school name on the front of the jersey is much more important than his individual name on the back. Each has set short-term goals and worked harder than most to become an "I" player, but then immediately commits to unselfishly contribute to the common long-term team objective by reaching out and pulling each teammate up to a higher level.

CREATING A WINNING TEAM ECOSYSTEM

Both building a winning team and creating a championship dynasty require an all-inclusive, self-perpetuating "packaged program," and there is no greater example of this than an ecosystem. An ecosystem is the interdependent, delicately balanced interaction among specific elements, where, through a circular process, they recycle themselves again and again to keep the system functioning and flowing. Water in the oceans, lakes, and rivers evaporates; winds, barometric pressure, and temperature mix and mingle; clouds form; and it rains or snows to replenish the earth's precious water supply, only to begin the process again and again and again.

It's Mother Nature's way of teaching that what goes around comes around and is the mindset required to not only build a winning team, but also to create a championship dynasty. As in nature, creating a self-perpetuating circular cycle of ongoing success and long-term desired results in our individual and organizational worlds comes only when we establish an interdependent team ecosystem.

As I've worked with teams (both sports and corporate at all levels), I've concluded that team building is like an ecosystem — one thing begins the process, and every step is connected thereafter, until a circular plane is formed. Never is team building about a one-way, straight-line, linear plane. Action creates the good feeling, the magic, and contagious chemistry that triggers more passion, creativity, and imagination — not vice versa. And because it's a circular system, success breeds success, winning breeds more winning, and a long-term championship dynasty emerges as a result of it.

DYNASTIES

Whenever the topic of championship dynasties comes up in a conversation, the Chicago Bulls share the top of the list with the NHL Edmonton Oilers hockey team (who from 1984-88 won four out of five Stanley Cup World Championship titles with "I" players Wayne Gretzky, Mark Messier, Jari Kurri, Paul Coffey, Glenn Anderson, Grant Fuhr, and Kevin Lowe); the legendary NHL Montreal Canadians with 24 Stanley Cup titles; and the MLB New York Yankees (who have dominated professional baseball winning 26 World Series titles in 39 appearances and being the only team represented at every position in the Major League Baseball Hall of Fame.

The Chicago Bulls won the National Basketball Association World Championship for a "Three-Peat" in 1990-91, 91-92, and 92-

Michael Jordon then retired and they didn't win the next season. Jordon comes out of retirement but they had lost some team chemistry and didn't win it all that year.

However, in 1995-96 the Bulls became the greatest NBA team ever, winning an unprecedented 72 games and the World Championship for the fourth time in six years. The Bulls won the NBA title again in 1996-97 and in 97-98 for their second "Three-Peat," creating a championship dynasty of six championships over eight years.

Wait! In 2015 the Golden State Warriors won the NBA Championship and then in 2016, surpassed the Bull's record and won an unprecedented 73 regular season games to make them one of the greatest teams of all time. All because of the shared clarity of vision, cause, contribution and chemistry of each team player who is individually committed to living by all TEN Cs on and off the court.

DO 'I' PLAYERS CREATE THE DYNASTY?

Wayne Gretzky won the National Hockey League's "Art Ross Trophy" point -scoring title from 1981-87, and was only the third player in NHL history to score 50 goals in 50 games. Steph Curry won the NBA scoring title and was MVP of the league to lead his Warriors to the championship. And Michael Jordon won seven straight NBA scoring titles, was Defensive Player of the Year a few times and League MVP and All-Star more than any player in history.

Michael retired from the Bulls after the 1998 season. "I" Coach Phil Jackson took a year off and "I" players Scottie Pippen, Steve Kerr and "Best" player Dennis Rodman all went to other teams. Overnight the Bulls became horrible and the rebuilding was to begin.

If you're the owner what do you do? Find a new "I" coach who can assemble "I" assistant coaches. They then find the new "I" player they can begin to rebuild their franchise around. In 2000, the Bulls drafted Elton Brand out of Duke University who was named Co-Rookie of the year and the Bulls were on their way.

Brand has since been traded to the L.A. Clippers where he continues to be a star and the Bulls team chemistry and roster of "I" players has finally gotten to the point where they made it back into the NBA post season playoffs in 2005. Building a winning team one "I" player at a time takes time, and only with a commitment to assemble only "I" players, can you start a winning streak and create a dynasty.

A baseball team has nine players, but when a player is up to bat, he's up there alone. He either succeeds alone or helps the team, or he fails alone and hurts the team. Every team win or loss boils down to individual performance. But what does it take to make winning a constant thing?

The NBA's Karl Malone and John Stockton couldn't get the basketball championship for the Utah Jazz by themselves, and Michael Jordan didn't get it all by himself. Neither did two players for the L.A. Lakers named Shaquille O'Neal and Kobe Bryant win it by themselves, nor repeat MVP Tim Duncan win the NBA championship for San Antonio by himself!

Not even super star MVPs LeBron James, who is clearly unstoppable at every level of the game, or Steph Curry or Kevin Durrant who are equally dominant in their own shooting and defensive skill sets, could win a championship by themselves.

Before we can put our best foot forward to assist others, we must first have a best foot. Before we can effectively and passionately participate on a committee, in a cooperative learning group, or on a winning team, we must become strong. Without individual preparation, without specific goals, without the freedom to dream new dreams, imagine, risk, fail, and succeed, neither the team nor the world will move ahead. Remember, any one man fighting for his family is stronger, braver, and more passionate than ten hired soldiers.

And when you assemble enough of these 'I' Players on the same team it's amazing how one win turns into winning and dominating your competition until you create a dynasty organization based on a culture of excellence in all you do.

Yes, LeBron James, Chris Bosh and Dwayne Wade were hired guns to play for the NBA Miami Heat and won two championships, but that success was short lived because the organizational culture of drafting the right 'I' Players to continue this winning streak were not in place.

Contrast this with the World Champion Golden State Warriors who have created the required 'Culture of Excellence' with the expectation that their players are champions and role models both on and off the court.

Yes, in 2017 Kevin Durant was brought from the Thunder to join the team, and yes Durant was named the MVP of the NBA Finals. But the reason the Warriors have won the World

Championship several times, and will continue to win is because of the 'I' Players they choose to draft who automatically fit into their team and organizational culture as 'I' People! Steph Curry, Klay Thompson, Draymond Green, and Andre Iguodala (who on a team with Step Curry was voted the MVP of the NBA Finals in 2015) were all late round draft choices by the Warriors who were molded and groomed and 'raised' in the 'system' to believe and contribute in a specific way.

IS CHEMISTRY OVERRATED?

We must remember that chemistry is about making everybody else around you better. The NBA is filled with "best" players who have four or five Cs: Alan Iverson, Kobe Bryant, etc., who also can win scoring titles. But to be a "right" player who takes everyone to the next level, not just his teammates whom he is playing with, but players on the opposing team he is playing against, he must possess all eight Cs. Losing even one "I" player on a team or one "I" employee in a company screws up team chemistry and unless you can get it back (not with best but with right people), taking your organization to the ultimate level, consistently winning and becoming more of who you are is only wishful thinking.

THE OBJECT IS TO WIN EVERY TIME

Whoever said it's not whether you win or lose that counts, probably lost. At the end of the 64-team NCAA basketball tournament, only one team remains. It is crowned national champion. One winning team is what makes the tournament and title so significant. It's why they call it "March Madness."

Not to be confused with the statement, *it's not whether you win or lose, but how you play the game*, which is true. Let me clarify. How you play the game is determined by the amount of preparation — the "art of execution" that took place before the game began, and the amount of passion, emotion, intensity, hustle, and disciplined, concentrated execution you put into winning the game.

"It doesn't matter if you win or lose until you lose. You know you're a champion only when losing hurts worse than winning feels good."

Good losers are still losers. You don't work so hard to win — you work so hard because you don't want to lose. As I mentioned in the previous context of building a winning team, great, successful, championship-winning coaches say that if a player is going to quit, they want him to quit in practice, not during a game. That's why they make practice so hard.

EXCELLENCE ALL THE TIME

Creating a championship dynasty wouldn't be that unique of an objective or the exception to the rule of most organizations if every team member on every team committed to excellence. One of the three core values of the U.S. Air Force is Excellence In Everything You Do.

This means winning in every aspect of your life 24 hours a day seven days a week. You can't just turn excellence on and off: physically, mentally, spiritually, emotionally, financially, socially, family — in which area of your life do you want to lose?

In which area are you not becoming more of who you are and reaching your full potential? What's holding you back? By no means can we be perfect, but in the process of relentlessly pursuing perfection we attain excellence.

An overweight, out of shape genius who graduated first in his class and makes a ton of money, yet is not involved in his community and has become so caught up in his fame and fortune that he has no spiritual side and a family that has fallen apart, is a huge disconnect for me!

Where is the consistency? Why would anybody settle for being a total loser in any aspect of his life? Winning is not a sometime thing, it's an all -the -time thing. It's not just on a scoreboard; it's a way of thinking and believing; a way of life.

The object in business, sports, and family living is to win. If a business does not win by making a profit, everybody loses their job. When companies go out of business, the community deeply suffers from the loss of a tax base, unemployment straps the government, opportunities are lost, dreams are shattered, and relationships are ruined.

Winning at whatever game we are playing at home, at work, at school, or at play is and always will be the reason we do what we do. If you don't agree, take down the hoops at a Saturday morning pick-up basketball game and see how many guys stick around to run up and down the court just for exercise. Keeping score is important, and winning gives our effort significance. Unless we want to win, there is no reason to stretch or surround ourselves with people who can take us to a higher, better place than we can take ourselves. We can only win when we become part of a team that understands and shares this belief.

CHAPTER TWENTY

CREATING AND SUSTAINING A WINNING STREAK

All in all, coach John Pease has reminded us that building a winning team is exciting, but the pride and excitement soon fade unless we recognize the four ingredients necessary to sustain the winning team and create a long-term dynasty: 1) preparation, 2) work ethic, 3) trust, and 4) respect.

The first two lead to numbers 3 and 4. You build trust with teammates by doing things together. Before practice and after practice we expose our true commitment to discipline and doing the right thing simply because it's the right thing to do. Nothing is more important than trust. It eliminates doubt.

Respect comes when we do what no one else will do — when we push ourselves and stretch beyond discomfort. When people think of record-setting National Football League Hall of Fame wide receiver Jerry Rice of the San Francisco 49ers and Oakland Raiders, most think only of his amazing catches. But the respect of his teammates and others in the NFL comes from the fact that he is also a superb and fearless blocking receiver. He does what most superstar receivers will not do!

Every team is always looking for one or two Jerry Rice-type "I" players. The reason is simply because they are the only players on the team who really want you to throw it to them long when time is running out, or who want to be in the baseball batter's box when it's the bottom of the ninth, the bases are loaded, and the team is behind by one and has two outs. They are the ones in the organization who can handle stress the best.

I have two questions: Can we build a winning team and create a long-term championship dynasty if only a few of the players can handle these stressful predicaments? Yes. Can we create a championship dynasty if only a few of the players can handle the stress? No. The coaching questions in any pressure packed game situation are, "Who is going to make a play? Which one of you, because you're all prepared to step it up, is going to rise to the occasion because the opportunity to be a hero is now at your position in your part of the field?"

In order to create and sustain a winning streak, every single player must take himself to a higher level. When Jerry Rice scored a touchdown, what had to happen for him to score? The coach called a strategic play, the snap and exchange from the center to the quarterback was perfect, every lineman blocked, Rice ran a perfect route, the QB threw it on the money, Rice caught the ball, another teammate blocked down field, and so forth. To win and continually win requires everybody to become a championship "I" player.

BOTH LABOR AND MANAGEMENT MUST BE WINNERS

Yes, we win through association, and this definitely spills over into our commerce side of life because we are naturally attracted to well-run, classy organizations. Everybody from everywhere likes to do business with winners.

For a company to win and consistently be the brand of choice, both labor and management need to be committed to excellence in everything they do. This does not just happen by accident or circumstance. We must teach and train each other to be *right* and to do *right.*

Even with a successful limousine company (I owned KC Limo in Salt Lake City), the training and coaching of drivers is based on in-the-box principles of self -discipline and perception similar to what is used in coaching sports. Anybody can purchase vehicles and start a transportation company.

The secret is in attracting and hiring the *right* people to drive who will allow you to teach them the *right* way to do it. (I trust you noticed that the way I phrased this explanation put emphasis on the person, not the performance—emphasis on the *right* person behind the wheel, not on the action of driving.) A company that is "reputable," which means *winning* and *right,* and that produces profitability and long-term success because of loyal, repeat customers, has drivers who:

Take great pride in the way they look – always being well groomed, smelling good, and presenting themselves with manners and sophistication. People who hire a limo are actually paying to win through association and want to feel classy and sophisticated for the few hours they are with the driver and the car.

- Always know the customers by name and respectfully address them as Mr. or Ms.
- Always know when to talk and when to stay silent.
- Refrain from backing up as much as possible.
- Choose a driving lane and stay in it.

Make sure they are always the second fastest vehicle (or the third fastest if they are traveling in a group, including with a police car) going in their direction on the road.

TEAM THERMODYNAMICS

The word *teamwork* has been preached since Benjamin Franklin proclaimed, "We must all hang together or assuredly we shall all hang separately." And it has become so in vogue that we have stopped challenging its deepest ramifications. For example, committees are, by nature, timid. They are based on the premise of safety in numbers and are content to survive inconspicuously rather than take risks and move independently ahead.

Cooperative learning groups in schools sound wonderful but are often misused or overhyped. One outstanding child usually gets stuck carrying the load, and in the law of thermodynamics, the two extremes of temperature – high-achiever "hots" and low-achiever "colds" – eventually reach a common, average-achiever temperature. Sure, cooperative team learning teaches students to get along with people, but schools typically don't measure or evaluate teamwork.

Colleges and universities sort applicants by grades, test scores, and individual athletic or musical skills, not because they can compromise. Corporations stress team but then have their customer service representatives working by themselves on the phone, while department heads, managers, and executives get all the bonuses, promotions, and awards. In professional sports, the concept of teamwork is faltering, with so-called stars taking over games and team payrolls.

We can never forget that championships are still won by teams. Think about the 2002 NFL Super Bowl champion New England Patriots, who broke tradition and chose to be introduced at the beginning of the game, not as individual superstars like in every other previous Super Bowl, but as a group – one total group – altogether as one team. And they played the entire game as a team. Even the injured starting quarterback Drew Bledsoe put team before self and cheered on his replacement. And the Patriots kept winning—three out of four Super Bowls, to be exact.

THE FRANCHISE 'I' PLAYER

Every team that wins regular season games cannot win the championship without a leader – without a winner, a standout star. Every championship team must have a franchise player who can carry the team on his shoulders for a lot of minutes and sometimes for entire games.

For example, remember quarterback John Elway in the last minutes of the famous drive to win the championship game between the Denver Broncos and Cleveland Browns, or Roger Craig carrying or catching the football nine times in the final minutes of the championship game to *will* and *make* the San Francisco 49ers go eighty yards to win? Craig was the first NFL running back (four Pro Bowls, three Super Bowl rings) to rush for a thousand yards and receive for a thousand yards in the same season!

Other examples include: Joe Montana to Dwight Clark for "the Catch" that beat the Dallas Cowboys; Franco Harris and his last play "Immaculate Reception" to score the winning touchdown for Pittsburgh against Oakland; Michael Jordan and Wayne Gretzky in the last four minutes of nearly every game or match they played. In the three Super Bowls the New England Patriots won, the winner was the young second-string quarterback, Tom Brady. Brady was an "I" player.

He proved that you don't need two "I" players at the same position.

Bledsoe was subsequently traded to the Buffalo Bills and then acquired for big bucks by the Dallas Cowboys, who needed an "I" player. In 2006, the Pittsburgh Steelers beat the Seattle Seahawks in the Super Bowl with big Ben Roethlisberger as their second-year, young but mature and composed "I" player QB. And Ben wasn't even the Super Bowl MVP! Hines Ward, his awesome receiver, was!

LITTLE THINGS MATTER

In order to truly inspire and coach "I" players to win a championship, we must pay attention to detail. I would never put anyone down to try to make myself appear better than I am. It's a sure sign of insecurity. But to make my point clear, how many young people who fail or get embarrassed spout the popular, "Oh, whatever"?

As if excellence and desired results suddenly don't matter? And how many of us adults are equally guilty when we make a mistake and blurt out, "Don't sweat the small stuff"? When anything negative happens, we suddenly rationalize, "Relax, get over it, it's no big deal, chill, don't blow it out of proportion, it's only one thing, only an employee, only a contract, only a game, a job" and so forth.

When we don't pay attention to the small stuff, it eventually turns into the cancerous, most painful, negative, destructive, biggest stuff of all. Germs ruin more vacations than bad weather, bad service and lost luggage combined.

Category-four Hurricane Charlie started in the Atlantic ocean when two small winds — one hot, one cold — that started blowing into each other until they swirled into a tropical storm and collided long enough to generate 150- mile-per-hour winds and weather conditions so violent the storm did billions of dollars in damage.

Hitler started out as a young ambitious man with a tyrant's dream bent on getting elected. America and Western Europe are great and free because we stopped him. I wonder what the history of the world would read if we had stopped Stalin in the Soviet Union, Pol Pot in Cambodia, Milosevic in Serbia and Saddam Hussein in Iraq before they massacred millions?

PEBBLE IN THE SHOE

The Grand Teton had turned him on each year
Prepared to climb her fourteen thousand feet of fear
He started out determined, to make his dream come true
And no it's not the boulder rocks that made him stop and get the blues

It was the pebble in the shoe, yeah the pebble in the shoe
A tiny thing that rubs us raw 'til it cuts through
A mighty clock will stop 'cause of one little screw
A rock chip in the windshield will soon crack through
Yeah David killed Goliath with a slingshot, true
With a stone, no bigger, than a pebble in the shoe

Some sell their 'Cedes, cause one cheap part breaks down
Some sell their piano, cause one key's flat in sound
Some throw the baby out, with the dirty water, true
But it's not that all is wrong, that causes fools to get blue...

It was the pebble in the shoe, yeah the pebble in the shoe
A tiny thing that rubs us raw 'til it cuts through

A mighty clock will stop 'cause of one little screw
A rock chip in the windshield will soon crack through
Yeah David killed Goliath with a slingshot, true
With a stone, no bigger, than a pebble in the shoe

They say don't sweat the small stuff, but the small stuff is the clue
You gotta fix the little things, before they fix you
Most start their love with vows, and promise they'll stay true
And no it's not the stumbling blocks that broke true love in two
It was the pebble in the shoe, yeah the pebble in the shoe

A tiny thing that rubs us raw 'til it cuts through
A mighty clock will stop 'cause of one little screw
A rock chip in the windshield will soon crack through
Yeah David killed Goliath with a slingshot, true
With a stone, no bigger, than a pebble in the shoe.

—Dan Clark copyright 2000

CHAPTER TWENTY-ONE

BEFORE WE CAN FIX OUR ORGANIZATIONS WE MUST FIX OURSELVES

Too often we forget that you can surgically remove the stripes from a tiger, and it's still a tiger. A geographic relocation doesn't change much. No matter where you go, there you are.
—Robert Pedersen

Justice without strength is helpless; strength without justice is tyrannical – unable to make what is just strong, we have made what is strong just. —Blaise Pascal

Winning a war is the reason we get into any conflict, period. Anything short of that is not acceptable. Second place in war means death. Anything worth starting is worth finishing and anything worth doing is worth doing right.

Winning at home, at work, at school, and at play is the reason we do what we do. If you don't agree, take down the hoops on a Saturday morning pickup basketball game and see how many guys stick around to run up and down the court just for exercise.

Keeping score is important, and winning gives our effort significance. Unless we want to win there is no reason to stretch or surround ourselves with people who can take us to a higher, better place – to the ultimate level where we can consistently win.

Heretofore we have defined winning, learned how to build a championship team and create a dynasty, and have delved into the specific psychology required to help any organization consistently win.

WHAT ABOUT LOSING?

We all have heard the countless excuses for why we lose, but what about the *reasons* we lose? Yes, this is a touchy subject for anyone who has lost, but the things we hate to hear the most are usually the things we need to hear the most.

Rather than avoiding the discussion and placing blame on others, it's time to remind each other that when we point our index finger at someone, our other three fingers are pointing straight back at us.

This discussion is simply a wake -up call to find out if the person we are really is the person we need to be. If not, then what to do about it. Emerson wrote, "Our chief want is someone who will inspire us to be what we know we could be."

The challenge in leadership is that when you are the big wig, top dog, head honcho, or championship winning coach, there are very few who are there to push and pull and inspire, lead, guide, coach and mentor you.

"Mentoring A Mentor"

The NFL Oakland Raiders are a classic example of the need for mentoring at the top. Of the many owners of professional sports teams, Mr. Al Davis is not only a shrewd businessman, but he is a generous human being, he was a loving tender companion to his sweet wife when she was ill, and is one of my personal heroes. But do you think his management methods and team building strategy are a little different?

As a maverick owner he is famous for going after misfits and paying them big bucks to do something they cannot do. You can take the girl out of the country but you can't take the country out of the girl. With all due respect, you can't win with losers. You can't have "me, me" renegades leading the NFL in penalties every year and expect them to play together for all twenty-four hours during the pre, regular, and post season.

Yes, I said hours not games. It takes only twenty- four hours to win the Super Bowl. Each game is sixty minutes long, and there are four preseasons, sixteen regular, and four playoff games. You would think anybody could stay fired up, stay focused and exercise poise, commitment, and discipline for twenty-four hours, but not the Raiders.

Mr. Davis is famous for saying and having signs put up around training camp, in the locker room, in the stadium and all over the East Bay, that claim the entire Raiders organization including the owner, GM, coaches and each and every player, have a "Commitment To Excellence." Mr. Davis is also famous for saying, "Just Win Baby!"

It means nothing and has not worked for years because he continually tries to coach results instead of behavior. Sometimes that works in the short term with the adrenaline rush of the moment, but it seldom works for twenty-four consecutive games.

So what happened to the Oakland Raiders in the 2016 season where they finished second in the AFC West? Under new coach Jack Del Rio they created a new and different culture of "Commitment To Excellence - Just Win Baby" by changing the expectations and drafting and trading for the 'right people,' who also happen to be some of the right 'I' players in the league. Because of this change in culture the Raiders improved from a 7- 9 win/loss record in 2015 to a 12-4 record and clinched a playoff birth for the first time since 2002.

Why? How? The Raiders signed the role model 'I' player quarterback Derek Carr and built around his amazing character and personal commitment to living by all Ten 'C' Commitments. Yes the Raiders lost this playoff game because Carr was injured and did not play. However, to sustain this new culture the Raiders re-signed Carr in 2017 making him the highest paid player in NFL history - a five year $125-million-dollar contract - earning $25 million a year!

Yes, becoming an 'I' Player pays off in both the short term and long run!

"The Exponential Multiplying Power Of 'I' Players"

In the 2006 NFL season the amazing NFL record-setting Peyton Manning and his Indianapolis Colts were undefeated in the regular season at 9-0, and nobody thought they could lose. The talk was Super Bowl champs and perhaps a perfect undefeated season. They then lost four games in a row with their run defense suddenly falling apart and their amazing receiving corps dropping easy passes.

I won't point fingers at specific players or casually slam the offensive line, because Peyton was running for his life on most third down conversions. But something was causing the team to unravel other than the teams they were playing against, and egos aside, the internal cause needed to be identified and repaired immediately or their season was over.

History shows they fixed what was broken. The Colts' defense ranked last against the run during the season, but became an amazingly strong and impenetrable curtain in the four playoff games including the Super Bowl where they dominated the Chicago Bears to become World Champions.

The real surprise was that the Bears' defense was one of the best of all time and yet the Colts' offensive line also stepped it up and dominated them as well. More specifically on this "mentoring" note, not only did the team as a whole take it to the ultimate level, but each individual "I" player stepped it up. Quarterback/captain Peyton Manning phoned fellow quarterbacks and former Super Bowl MVPs Brett Favre, Tom Brady, and John Elway to find out what they did differently and how they prepared their teams to win the big one. What worked for them worked for Peyton Manning and the Colts. Will it always work?

"Amateurs Practice Until They Get Better – Pros Practice Until They Don't Miss"

Even though the Raiders played in Super Bowl 2, won Super Bowls 11, 15, and 18 (in 1984), they didn't appear again until 2003 – Super Bowl 37 – where they got drilled by Tampa Bay. What happened?

Two days before the biggest game of his life, one of the starting, yet misfit, rebel, maverick lineman went AWOL and missed meetings, practice, and press time. Consequently, he was suspended from playing in the game, ensuring that the Raiders would self-destruct again. And he was supposedly one of the leaders, as his teammates counted on him to call the audible adjustments at the line of scrimmage.

In fact, nothing happened on offense until he snapped the ball making him the key to every play. Yes, you can have the *best* misfit in the world, but it's only a matter of time, not if, but when he will flip out and let himself and his teammates down.

Maybe you're cringing, saying, cut the man some slack, give a brother another chance, and what about being there for the troubled ones? Obviously there are exceptions to the rule left to our empathetic judgment. But on a championship winning team we don't practice just to get better, we practice to never miss winning the championship again.

Bottom line? It's impossible for anyone to fix another human being. We can fix organizations and processes and change out individuals on the team, but when it comes to human resource management, the only person we can fix is ourselves.

For this reason, no one can teach anyone anything. As we have stated, only when the student is ready will the teacher appear. We can't teach others, but we can learn all we want when we want! We can't motivate others. We can only inspire them to motivate themselves.

As mentioned throughout this leadership education experience, what the players do when the coaches are not around really does make or break them. Once the game begins the coaches are stuck on the sideline. Besides calling the offense and defensive alignments and yelling, "Who is going to make a play?" the coaches are helpless when extra effort, hustle, character, mutual respect, support, and love are needed on the field to get the first down or cause a turnover to win.

The same thing holds true for coaches while coaching. Once the game starts it is too late to decide in a non-emotional environment what the play calling flow will be; what you will say and how you will say it to rally your fellow coaches and players if you fall behind; how and why you will save and use your sacred timeouts; what unique play or unexpected screen pass you will run to get out of bounds and manage the clock wisely; what the two-minute offense will specifically be to put points on the board quickly; and whether or not you will go for two to win.

FACING THE BRUTAL FACTS OF REALITY

For all of these reasons, this is the blunt chapter that invites you to face the brutal facts of your reality. Although most of the readers of this book are not coaches, I choose to internally excavate the mindset and personality of a coach as the source of this study for all of us. Why coaches?

Sports psychologists all concur that the coaching profession draws into it a very unique personality. Not everybody can be a coach, and out of the select men and women who actually get the opportunity, there are only a few who become best enough to win – fewer who become right enough to win championships. What makes these individuals different? The experts who study them simply explain:

Successful Coaches Are "Control Freaks!"

Anyone who is willing to showcase their strengths and weaknesses, put their win/loss record out in the public eye to be constantly evaluated, and their family on display subject to ridicule when they lose, always wants to control everything he/she possibly can.

Look around. Look at yourself. Coaches who win are extraordinarily anal about controlling who plays, what they play, when they play, the plays called, the defenses run, time outs, player curfew, off-field behavior by establishing consequences, on field-behavior through example and class, and even the design of uniforms and coaches garb!

By the nature of the beast, coaches think they know it all, try to do it all, tie their self-esteem into the success and failure of their team, and have a tough time admitting they are wrong. Consequently, a lousy coach is extremely difficult to fix. It's why when coaches do poorly over even a short period of time they are fired instead of given another chance.

This is also why the previous scenario about the coach waiting until game time to make critical decisions makes so much sense. When the game starts it is too late for a coach to take control. And because they are control freaks, when they lose control, they lose!

"Knowing What Not To Fix"

Is there anything that can be done to help us coaching types see the light before our team goes down the tube? Absolutely. It begins with knowing what to control, micromanage and fix and what to macro manage and leave alone. For example, legendary UCLA basketball coach John Wooden is famous for his foremost emphasis on fundamentals.

With a reputation as the ultimate control freak "my way or the highway," his fanatical discipline brought him ten National NCAA College Basketball Championships. Interesting when you know that one of his all-time greatest players, Jamal Wilkes, nicknamed "Silk," had the quirkiest, most unconventional shot ever imagined.

His elbow stuck out to the side and he shot the ball from behind his head. When asked why he didn't spend time teaching Wilkes the "best" and conventional shooting technique of keeping his elbow down and parallel to his torso and releasing the ball in front of his face, ultra-conservative coach Wooden smiled and replied, "How Jamal shoots is irrelevant. He is an All-American who scores over 20 points a game. Maybe his method is right and everybody else is wrong?"

As long as our 'how-to' is always 100 percent honest, honorable, and ethical, the means can justify the end. As in life, the goal in basketball is to put the ball in the basket more times than your opponent does. Who cares if it's the best way or how it looks going in? **Scoring ugly is still scoring**. The question is not how many storms you encountered along your way, but did you bring in the ship?

Do you agree? If so, how will you know what to fix and what to ignore? And let us not forget the fact that before we can ever fix what is broken in an organization, we must acknowledge what is broken in ourselves and commit to doing that which is necessary to change and be successful. According to my colleague and bestselling author Bob Kriegel, sometimes "if it ain't broke, we need to break it."

Study the following test. Then with sincere candor decide if you are, or are not broken, or need to be "broke." Psychologists call this self-audit evaluation the "Competency Exam."

CHAPTER TWENTY-TWO

THE FOUR COMPETENCIES OF HUMAN PERFORMANCE

UNCONSCIOUS INCOMPETENT

They don't know that they don't know.
Clueless. No Hope.

A good example would be a child who has never seen a bicycle, or has no idea that any language exists other than their own.

CONSCIOUS INCOMPETENT

They know they don't know.
Teachable. Hopeful.

An example might be the child who has seen other children riding bicycles, or heard someone speaking another language, and therefore wishes to learn.

CONSCIOUS COMPETENT

They first take time to learn the facts and know truth and right, but they must think about it and concentrate before doing it.

An example would be the child who can ride a bicycle but falls off if they stop watching where they are going.

UNCONSCIOUS COMPETENT

They know the facts, truth and right, and do the right thing without thinking about it. Through repetition they have taken their performance to a deeper subconscious/unconscious level.

They understand discipline to mean "minding a set of rules administered by another," and understand self-discipline to mean "minding yourself." In any positive or negative situation, they automatically rise to the occasion and naturally respond in a good, clean, pure, powerful, positive, productive way to do the right thing simply because they can.

An example would be the child who no longer has to think about how they ride the bike, but just do it. In fact, if they think about it too hard, they may not be able to do it.

A Metaphorical Story

In which competency do you fall? Do you know someone who is ever learning and never able to come to a knowledge of the truth; who suffers so badly from the paralysis of analysis that he overthinks everything because simple solutions don't satisfy his ego's need to feel more intelligent than others?

I know this competency question is relevant depending on which area of your life I am asking about, but generally speaking, with 100 percent honesty, are you an unconscious competent? If you are in an influential leadership position as a manager, educator or coach, anything less is unacceptable.

Using our affirmation that the "answers are still in the box," (which means everything we need to take ourselves and our organizations to the next level is already inside of us), let us use the metaphor of four walls fastened together and stabilized with four cornerstones, with the floorboard base bottom of the box being *unconscious competency*.

Because everything rests and relies on it, answering whether or not you are an *unconscious competent* must be more than just a casual yes or no. Therefore, I present to you a story wherein you can plug yourself into the various characters and scenarios and honestly answer how you would have responded. I know this learning method works from a personal experience.

The Goal

During the 1980s, many of America's leading university MBA programs taught from a book called *The Goal*. It was a business novel written about a father trying to balance his personal life with managing employees, profits, and productivity. His toughest task was eliminating bottlenecks in his company's warehouse distribution system.

This text seemed irrelevant to the graduate students until their professors challenged them to read between the lines and figure out the lessons in the author's experiences, especially in the unique stories such as the father leading his young son's Boy Scout troop on a 20-mile hike, and what he learned about human resource management from the overweight kid who held everybody else up.

As with *The Goal*, this chapter may seem irrelevant to you. However, I too, challenge you to extract the many points made and to sharpen those points for your own use. We have discussed the causes of a team falling behind and losing, or coming from behind and winning a game, but we have yet to explain why a championship dynasty organization suddenly collapses and starts losing many games. What does it specifically take at the leadership level to stop the losing streak, recapture momentum and never let the nightmare happen again?

Although this is a story about a high school football program, reading this chapter in its entirety will allow you to internally excavate who you really are through the minds, competencies, personalities, and management styles of some coaches orchestrating a "season on the brink."

TITANS….. REMEMBER THE EAGLES!

I've been an assistant football coach at Skyline High School in Utah for six years. In the 30- year history of the Utah State Football Association, Skyline has played in 21 of the 30 state championship games. As of 2004, Skyline had won thirteen State 5A championships and has been ranked as high as fifteen in the national *USA Today* poll.

Their legendary head football coach, Roger Dupaix, who has ten children and has been happily married for over 25 years, has been coaching football for over 35 years, has over 265 wins – most by any active coach in Utah, has been named Coach of the Year numerous times, and was enshrined into the National College Football Hall of Fame in 2005.

While Coach Dupaix was named Utah's Coach of the Decade, Skyline's football program was being honored as the Utah High School Program of the Century! Whoa. Go Eagles!

At the beginning of every season, Coach Dupaix strengthens our team unity by linking our new team to the winning traditions of past champions. He passionately shares his expectations that we will again win the state championship if we will just dedicate ourselves to thinking, believing, working, sacrificing and doing exactly what the past champions have done.

Coach Steve Marlowe, offensive backfield/special teams coach and one of the finest Athletic Directors in America, then gives our players the unity speech that every individual will now be labeled a Skyline football player and will not be separated from this distinction until they graduate. Every individual act from here on out affects the entire team – all for one and one for all in every sense of the word. If you get in a fight, or get caught cheating or stealing, the newspaper headline will read, "Skyline football player was arrested."

Coach Marlowe's first of the season speech always encourages every student athlete to walk on higher ground; that everybody is watching them and therefore, they should go out of their way to be gentlemen; say please and thank you; go to class and support all other extracurricular activities in the school from drama, music, debate, and especially the girl's sporting events.

Year in and year out, regardless of our record, the football players at Utah's Skyline High School are some of the classiest young men in the entire world! Assistant coaches Justin

Thompson, Kenny James, John Frank, Jackson Peck, Craig VanLewen, Brodie Reid, and Beau Marlowe are not only outstanding coaches, but they are great human beings and super role models for our young men to watch, interact with, and be around.

What Works, Works

In 2005, Skyline won its fourteenth state championship in an extraordinary way. The team lost a combined five pre - season and regular-season games, finishing fourth place in its region with a three and five record. The team barely made it into the state playoffs and was expected to be eliminated in the first game. Skyline was drilled and beaten by as many as thirty points in losses during the season and yet won all four playoff games in a row to win the state championship.

The championship game was against archrival Brighton High School, which had beaten Skyline during the regular season. Sports writers, coaches, parents, and fans are still asking me how we did it. What was our secret? What miraculously changed our team from losers into winners, from mercenaries into missionaries, from mediocre into *right best* players?

Let me give you the thorns and roses. Among the many lessons learned that I will detail in this segment, the seven most fundamental truths that apply not only to coaching sports, but to parenting, teaching, leading, and managing people in a corporate, educational, military and/or business setting are:

- People don't like to be told what to do – especially young people.

- People don't like to feel stupid or embarrassed. You praise in public and chastise in private.
- You can't increase a person's performance by making him feel worse. Humiliation immobilizes behavior.
- Discipline is to teach, not to punish. We have chosen coaching as our vehicle to help boys and girls turn into men and women; to help everyone around us go from good to great, move from great to best, and transform from best into right – both on and off the field of play.
- Never give an assignment without first giving proper and complete training. Remember, most people don't have a learning disability. They have a learning difference. If anything we have a teaching disability. We must test for understanding before we expect execution.

Using the "Forward Thinking" teaching model is key. Instead of telling and showing the player/employee what they did wrong, you move forward and never put that negative image in their mind again. Why reinforce a thought or behavior that you don't want repeated by doing it again?

Too many coaches turn on the previous game film and yell, "You idiot, how many times do I have to tell you? Don't do this, don't do that. Look at how you screwed up there!" The "forward thinking" coach says, "If you want to sack the quarterback or pass block, or break through the line and run for a touchdown, this is exactly how and why and when you do it; this is what you do with your hands, feet, butt, head, body, this is the angle you must take, and these are the specific stretching, weight lifting and reaction drill exercises you must do and practice on your own time in order for your thinking and behavior to become automatic which is the only way you can make this team.

Don't confuse activity with accomplishment. Putting in practice time doesn't guarantee game time wins. We must do the right thing AND do things right.

Legendary University of Alabama and College Football Hall of Fame coach Paul "Bear" Bryant reiterates these seven people-building truths in his answers to three interview questions. When asked if the rumor was true that he walked on water and therefore, didn't really have to spend much time on the job, he smiled and said, "I won't say I can or can't; but if I do, I do it before most people get up in the morning."

When asked about his approach to dealing with a loss, Coach Bryant explained, "Most coaches study the films when they lose. I study them when we win, to see if I can figure out what I did right." When asked about discipline, Coach Bryant quoted U.S. President Theodore Roosevelt: "Obedience of the rules and the law is demanded; not asked as a favor." Coach concluded, "Listening, thinking, studying, working, hustling, and doing whatever is required to prepare to win, both for coaches and players, is not an option."

Learn From Others' Mistakes

These and other thorny truths and the blatant disregard for their consequences became evident during the regular season of 2005, when the high -strung defensive coaches usually caught players doing things wrong. Some coaches were so caught up in their "turf" and who was right rather than what was right, that they openly fought and loudly argued among themselves in front of the team.

Defensive line coach John Franks, another former Skyline player who went through the system, was Mountain West Conference Defensive Player of the Year for the University of Utah, and went on to play for the NFL Philadelphia Eagles. He was the only constant, mellow, voice of unconditional love and reason on the defensive practice field.

Consequently, because players were in constant fear of getting yelled at they were never able to get in touch with their football instincts and free up their amazing natural athletic abilities.

The defensive coordinator, genius coach Steve Marshall, whose vast knowledge, extraordinary analytical mind, award-winning years playing in high school, college, and in the NFL, coupled with the thousands of hours and over 30 years he's spent coaching, easily makes Steve one of the top ten high school coaches in America.

But as a new defensive coordinator, when he decided to let each position coach do his own thing, hoping that at game time, everyone would play together, even though the end result was agreed upon, the methodology and techniques used to execute the defense was different for each position, and the conflict between coaches continued to escalate as the season progressed.

When we lost, everybody blamed everybody but themselves. "I told you so" was the nonverbal communication among us. It was clear that we had players playing in the wrong positions, but to remain politically correct, no coach made the necessary moves.

Players were uneasy, insecure, and intimidated. But during the playoffs, things suddenly changed to liking to be around each other, mutual respect, and open communication, with coaches catching players and each other doing things right! What was the magic formula?

Can other coaches on other teams duplicate what we did? Will what the Skyline coaches did work and apply to the professional corporate business world? Was it leadership or management or both? Was it coaching or playing?

CHAPTER TWENTY-THREE

OUR COACHES MORPHED THROUGH ALL FOUR COMPETENCIES

COACHES WERE UNCONSCIOUS INCOMPETENTS

Because some of the coaches didn't know that they didn't know, they were clueless and there was no hope to turn the season around. Obviously before you can fix what's broken, you must first realize something is broken. When things haven't gone as you expected, yet you still had a pretty good season, it's easier to overlook what's broken and just move on. Most coaches would rationalize and say, "Wait until next year." But Skyline football coaches are not like most coaches. However, we are like most people.

Finding fault in the players and their execution was far easier than finding fault in ourselves as a coaching staff.

In my opinion and eyewitness observation, we lost five games this season and championships from years past because of one major weakness. Certain coaches thought some of our players had learning disabilities when, in reality, they had teaching disabilities. They talked fast and expected these young men to catch on in the first explanations. They bad-mouthed and benched those who did not.

One classroom teacher/coach always graded players by their smarts and test scores calling lower academic achievers stupid. I found that ironic in that the NFL with the best football players on the planet tested their players and discovered that the average reading level in professional football is at the seventh grade level!

C'mon coach. If the player doesn't immediately comprehend and remember the complicated defense you have spent hours figuring out and years to perfect, you label him too slow and unfit to play for you? When I challenged a coach about this apparent team-wide communication disconnect, he got defensive and yelled, "What do you mean? I have worked hard and given everything I have to coach these boys."

I thought, "True, but irrelevant if you are confusing activity with accomplishment. We are losing games Bubba, and something is causing it besides the teams we play!" I worked with the "scout team" every day and saw the tough, strong, hardworking boys who never got to play, who only needed a little extra one- on-one coaching and a chance in a game to show what they could do and they would have been awesome starters!

But they never got their chance. This is unacceptable and has always hurt our team, especially when one of the "favored few" gets injured and we suddenly need a game-tested replacement.

This year it was different. Our offensive line coach, Kenny James, has volunteered his time for many years, and as the head Junior Varsity coach set a Utah state winning streak record. Kenny's extraordinary understanding of the wishbone offense and his passion and love of the game was so contagious that our offensive linemen all got along, loved each other, worked hard and stood out as a tightly knit group of warriors fighting for each other.

Sam Walton, Plant, Carlson and the rest will always stand out in Skyline lore. Sadly, they were the only ones. Having only a few *right* players isn't enough to create a winning championship team. Yes, most of our guys had most of the "Ten Cs" of building a winning team, but we were still losing.

COACHES BECAME CONSCIOUS INCOMPETENTS

The answer to our turnaround was simple and obvious. Coaches became humble and teachable and finally knew that they didn't know. All in all, we finally got the right players, playing the right positions at the right place on the field at the right time with the right understanding of the plays, attitude, focus, mental toughness, and physical fitness to execute perfectly and get the job done.

Second, it suddenly was no longer about the coaches and what they thought was the *best* way. It became about the players and the *right* way. For the first time all season, the coaches made sure everybody got it before they moved on. Even our second string players and scout team squad took pride in their practice performance, knew our plays and felt a part of the team!

COACHES BECAME CONSCIOUS COMPETENTS

The birth into the state tournament gave us coaches a new lease on life, allowing us to seize a second chance to fix our tarnished pride, egos, and reputations and demonstrate our knowledge, experience, and love for the game. We took the time to learn the facts and know the truth and right, although we still had to think about it and concentrate before doing it.

For the first time in the year, it was no longer about us or for us. It was 100 percent only for the players, their families, and our school. The horrible regular season record was a shocking wake-up call that life is not about *me* – it's about others.

The defenses were so complicated that the younger players were confused while the coaches were caught up in their superiority complex. But by playoff time the coaches had finally been humbled enough to realize the interdependence of everyone in our organization. In one day, the coaches remembered that we can get anything in this life that we want if we are just willing to help enough other people get what they want.

When we serve others, a lot of crumbs fall off the table for us. When the water in the lake goes up, all boats rise together. All for one and one for all – one heartbeat, one dream.

COACHES FINALLY BECAME UNCONSCIOUS COMPETENTS

Ironically, in the midst of huge egos who had a right to believe they knew it all because they had previously done it all, a new assistant coach in his first year on our staff, spoke up in our coaches meeting and changed the feeling in the room. Suddenly it was a "love fest" where each coach expressed his respect and admiration for each other and how much coaching together really meant to us!

In retrospect, I honor this young man, Coach Jackson Peck, who in this meeting humbly made the suggestion to simplify the defense into the system that he had run as an award winning college safety. Amazingly everyone agreed, and Coach Peck's enthusiasm spread through the coaching staff and into every player on the team.

Knowing the facts and the truth and right, we started doing the right thing without thinking about it. Through spaced repetition we took our communication and mutual respect and support for each other and toward the players to a deeper subconscious/unconscious level where in any situation we were able to automatically rise to the occasion and make the right decision for the benefit of everybody.

In all my years, in all my travels, and in all my experiences working with the NFL, NCAA, and other high school coaches and sports teams, I've never seen a coaching staff get more serious and intense and spend more hours auditing themselves, forgiving each other, watching more film, documenting more tendencies of each new opponent, and developing a competitive mental edge than this Skyline High School 5A football state championship team's coaching staff did in the 2005 season!

In particular, Coach Justin Thompson, a product of the system as a former player at Skyline, put together our scouting report each week. During the regular season, he put in an average of thirty hours per week, but during the playoffs increased it to sixty hours to take our scouting reports to an amazing detailed level.

When the playoffs began, all of our football coaches were sacrificing all of their free time and every aspect of their social lives. They were doing absolutely everything they knew how to do to better prepare themselves and take the entire organization to the next level.

Coach Marshall has always preached team first and winning the championship over winning individual honors. Even he was practicing this more than he had ever preached. This revitalized dedication of the coaches strengthened the trust of the players, which inspired them to also step it up, put team first, watch more film, study their new playoff playbooks, memorize the improved scouting reports, get more sleep, focus on the snap count, concentrate on eliminating penalties, sacrifice their social lives, and perfect their execution.

During the season we had countless penalties and jumped off sides in every game. In the four state playoff games we did not jump off sides once and averaged only one penalty per game. Mental toughness and focus on purpose, backing it up with work ethic for coaches *and* players makes a coach and a player *right*.

KISS – KEEP IT SIMPLE SKYLINE

As I mentioned, after we got ourselves and our players *right*, the only other thing left was to simplify our offense and defense and get back to what we do best. Our offense is a wishbone running scheme, throwing the ball usually only three times a game.

During the season we threw it ten to fifteen times a game—unsuccessfully. Our defensive coaches are former all-conference, All-American, or NFL players; consequently, they approached each game plan from that state of mind. We forgot we were dealing with young boys—eleven starters on this 2005 team being 16-year-old eleventh graders.

As an assistant coach for so many years, somehow I became the designated "catholic-priest-type-confession-counselor guy" whom the parents called and confidentially complained to about how their sons were being mistreated. I was also the trusted confidant of the discouraged players who needed some inspiration and someone to talk to.

This particular year the young men were overwhelmed by how much the coaches disagreed, and were scared to death to ask any questions about the confusing defenses the coaches kept changing each week. I had mentioned these concerns at coach's meetings on a couple of occasions, but because of their "don't mess with my turf," "Look how much success I've had in the past so you don't know what you're talking about" driven egos, they shot me down claiming "former players got it so these boneheads should too."

But isn't it amazing how five losses in a row at season's end can humble even the most hardened veterans to finally realize that success is not about programs and playbooks until it's about principles and people willing to fix themselves, admit their faults, and make critical adjustments before it's too late?

CHAPTER TWENTY-FOUR

BUSINESS/EDUCATIONAL/MILITARY LESSONS LEARNED

Absolutely create a climate of mutual respect and support at the highest level between fellow executives/the entire coaching staff, where it is safe, welcome, and expected to offer suggestions and corrections, regardless of age, race, sex, or years of experience.

Every business should have an anonymous suggestion box to collect honest feedback, constructive criticism, and positive praise on how to better run the organization. (In this case it was the players begging for a less complex defensive strategy). Once the employees know that leadership really does listen and learn, this trusting relationship becomes the foundation on which company executives can solicit every employee – custodians, secretaries, sales agents, assembly line laborers, manufacturing foreman, warehouse distribution managers, customer service reps, engineers, accountants, account managers, anyone – to come up with a brand new invention, better system or way, or a more innovative application of an existing product, and then compensate them for it.

Hewlett Packard, IBM, Georgia Pacific, and many other extraordinary companies have had some of their best selling products invented by an employee who in turn, is paid huge dollars for their ideas and solutions. A win/win for everybody and the entire team benefits because of one!

It's never too late to begin to build a winning team – after a terrible first quarter profit and loss, short-of-projected-earnings revenue report, at midyear after a miserable start, at the beginning of the playoffs after a barely good-enough-to-get-in season, or at the end of the year because you finally realize if best is possible good is not good enough.

It's never too late to stop focusing on who is right as individuals, and start focusing on what is right for the team.

We focused only on what we could do—refusing to let what we could not do interfere with what we could. Companies that fail do so for the same reason in that they get sidetracked from their core business. We fixed a lot of things by simply becoming great at what we could be great at! Once we finally admitted who we were, evaluated our talent, and recommitted to being brilliant at the basics, we proactively turned things around.

Skyline won because we again affirmed who we were. If you're a wishbone team, you run and run and perfectly execute the wishbone. Duh! A coach's job is to create opportunities and put players in situations where they can best succeed—not for their own glory but for the benefit of the team. Once they succeed, success breeds success, and their energy and confidence increase.

Yes, we won the final game in a come-from-behind victory (down 24-10 at halftime) but rallied back to be crowned Utah State 5A Champions and win 34-24. Because of this newly created culture and feeling of unconditional love, mutual respect and true tangible "family togetherness," individual players stepped up their game and together won the championship one play at a time. I honor our All-Region and All-

State superstars: quarterback Matt Marshall, the entire offensive line, running backs Kalama Molisi, James Johansen, Toa Taeoalii, offensive/defensive lineman Brian Vaaulu, utility player Chase Pendley, linebacker Ben Marlowe, and safety Jason Hanks.

2006 SEASON UPDATE

With eleven starters back, the defense simplified and fortified, and with most of the coaching ego challenges resolved, I'm sure you are expecting me to report that Skyline High School repeated as the Utah State 5A Football Champions.

No. We beat nationally ranked Las Vegas High School earlier in the season and had some moments of brilliance in a few games. However, we lost the last two games of the regular season when we were ahead in both games to barely get a third place entry into the state tournament. We then lost the first round game of the playoffs to an inferior opponent. Why?

Why were the NFL New England Patriots able to repeat as Super Bowl Champions three out of four years in a row, and not Skyline? We won 5 state championships in a row from 1995-1999. Why not repeat at least once again?

One of the most important things I thought we fixed from years past came back to haunt us again. Although the coaches got along, the lack of honest communication ruined our team. It was clear during our summer training camp before the season even got under way, that the wrong guys were playing in a couple of the most important positions. (Whoops! Apparently I have been jaded by the coaches more than I realized, and didn't mean to say this. Let me rephrase my observation.)

What I meant to say is that three of the "right" guys who could have been All-State safeties, linebackers, and lineman, were put at wrong positions that their personalities and superstar skills were not suited for.

DÉJÀ VU ALL OVER AGAIN

Coaches Became Unconscious Incompetents – Again!

We all know the definition of insanity and, in this case, stupidity, is doing the same thing and expecting a different result. The sad thing is, a coach's primary responsibility is to put a young man in a position that will give him a chance to personally succeed so he can help the team win, and one of these amazing young men was put in a position where at best he could be average.

I've seen this all over the country where the school superintendent's son is playing quarterback just because of who his daddy is, and the team loses because of it. I also saw the other side of this in an Oklahoma high school where they hired a legendary coach away from an extraordinarily successful Putnam City program to take over a losing program at Yukon.

The first thing coach "Mike" did was start moving the players into the positions they should have been playing all along. Yes he almost got fired in the first few weeks as some of the big name powerful boosters and parents were up in arms, but he did what he was hired to do and moved the school board member's son who had played quarterback since he was in little league to wide receiver and the tight end to tailback and the wide receiver to quarterback.

Long story short, they won the state championship. But enough of this documented outside proof, let's get back to my eyewitness Skyline account.

As mentioned, out of the pressure of personal politics, other players were also put into key roles who should not have been playing those positions either, but a coach had his favorites. I wanted to play a specific young man and the other coach wanted to play his guy and both had their strengths and weaknesses.

When my guy made a mistake he got yelled at. When his guy made a mistake he got questioned. Players notice little things like this and over time we lost the feeling of family togetherness and commitment to each other as "brothers-in-arms" required to fight back when we fell behind.

Not necessarily player to player, but player to coach and especially coach to coach. Unlike the year before when the coaches made all the difference, this time the coaches lost the championship for these young men and we should be forever ashamed of ourselves for not rising above such obvious pettiness and doing that which was necessary to succeed.

FINAL BUSINESS/EDUCATION/MILITARY APPLICATION

Be loyal to those who are not present; never give an assignment without first giving that individual the proper training; always give the person in charge the necessary authority to make decisions regarding his assignment and the people he is responsible for; remember that cancer is the worst disease and fastest spreading cause of failure in any organization and these type of sick individuals are seldom cured.

In sports, school, and business, sometimes it's better that one soul should parish than a whole organization dwindle in anger, intimidation and broken dreams. Anyone who is arrogant, pompous, disrespectful, and caught up in their own intelligence and self- imposed importance should be thinned from the heard – especially if he/she is a coach.

When coaches get their "turf" feathers ruffled and decide to communicate head-to-head to send a message of control, rather than heart to heart in a message of mutual respect and support so the entire staff can be of one mind and one cause, the negative ramifications are immediate.

Organizational Communications *101* teaches that hoarding and holding back information is one of the main reasons any team, corporation, and marriage relationship fails. It really is true. Before you can fix what is broken you must know what is broken, and sometimes "if it ain't broke, we should break it." The hardest thing is to fix yourself.

Because of this eye-opening experience at Skyline High, I now know you can have wrong people in the right program; get right answers to the wrong questions; put right players and employees in the wrong positions; recruit best coaches and managers to the wrong program; have best coaches and leaders be right about the wrong things; lose "I" coaches to the competition; and tarnish friendships between extraordinary human beings for the most ordinary reasons.

Even in business and sports, the goal is to make everybody else around us better, including the competition, and always leave the office, practice field and game in better shape than we found them.

Every coach in every sport, male and female, both amateur and professional, not just at Skyline High, but at every school and university and in every organization; as well as every corporate coach responsible for building a winning business, needs to remember:

The goal in every practice, game, office encounter at work, training meeting and every other time they are in your presence on task and off task, is to have people leave impressed with themselves, not intimidated by the coach – impressed with what they now know that they didn't know before; impressed with what they now can do that they could not do before; and positively encouraged, motivated and inspired by you to do it.

I guess it *is* true. Especially in coaching. You can't increase a person's performance by making him feel worse. If this discussion has ruffled your feathers, made you feel guilty and worse, I guess you now know how it feels. Don't shoot the messenger. And definitely don't think by getting away from me, or this message, or changing teams or companies will change things.

Remember, a geographic relocation doesn't change much of anything. No matter where you go, there you are. Be a control freak. Fix yourself. And if you don't think you're "broke" at all, most likely you need to break something! We all do! Case closed.

CHAPTER TWENTY-FIVE

YOU CAN'T QUIT – IT'S A LEAGUE RULE!

"Nothing in the world can take the place of persistence. Talent will not; nothing is more common than unsuccessful men with talent. Genius will not; unrewarded genius is almost a proverb. Education will not; the world is full of educated derelicts. Persistence and determination alone are omnipotent. The slogan 'Press On' has solved and always will solve the challenges of the human race." —Calvin Coolidge

In our highly competitive world, we must understand that there is nothing more insignificant than the halftime score! Succeeding from the inside out is not a sporadic, sometime, one quarter, first half thing that is out of our control. It is an all-the-time thing we can control. Have you never heard, "It's mind over matter – when your attitude is right your abilities will always catch up?"

When I played college football at the University of Utah, we took on UCLA. Before the game our coach pumped us up, saying, "UCLA has the biggest team in the nation and they are ranked in the top ten teams in the country. So what? They put on pants just like you do. Don't be afraid. UCLA doesn't have to win this game. Tonight is our night. You can win if you think you can. Just believe in yourselves. Go out and win!"

The game started. We got the ball first. They quickly took it away from us. It was now our turn to stop them. I should have been excited but the guy across the line from me was about 8 foot 92 and looked like he tipped the scales right around what a water buffalo would weigh! So big that I had to look through his legs to see what was going on. He easily could have kick-started a 747 jet!

When they hiked the ball, he hit me so hard that he knocked my helmet around my head so that I was looking out my ear hole. When I came to, I thought I had gone blind!

As I stood there bleeding and crying, it suddenly occurred to me that my coach was lying! *UCLA does have to win this game and I quit*, and I started to walk off the field. To my dismay the coach met me halfway, pointed toward my teammates, and pushed me back into the huddle.

Wouldn't you know it? The next play we sacked the quarterback. Actually, I did! I have to admit that I ran into him by accident, but I still tackled him for a loss. He fumbled the ball. We recovered. We scored. We stopped them again and again and scored twice more. UCLA's quarterback thought he was caught in one of those revolving doors at the mall. The halftime score was 19-0 in favor of the University of Utah. Yee Haw!

However, despite our great start and halftime lead, because we started thinking that somehow we weren't supposed to be beating UCLA and started questioning our ability to sustain this high level of play; and because the players for UCLA believed they were better than this, we lost our confidence, lost our momentum, and lost the game 23–19.

On another occasion we played the University of Oklahoma. On our first ball possession, we scored and were ahead, 7-0. Yes, we were whipping the Sooners! It was those last 59 minutes that killed us! We lost, 62-24.

In yet another game, this time with a different outcome, we were behind the University of Arizona at halftime, 21–0. By the end of the third quarter we were losing 27–0. During the last seconds of the game, however, we pulled it out, scoring at the buzzer to win 28-27!

FOCUS AND FINISH

The difference is in the fact that you can't coach results – you can only coach behavior. You can't tell your children to get good grades in school, your employees to sell more, your players to win the game, or your troops to defeat the enemy. You can only coach them to set high expectations and to put in the necessary practice time to improve their attitudes and confidence, and perfect their skills and behavior so that winning takes care of itself. The quickest way to comprehend all of the ramifications of this mindset and inspire our selves and others to stretch and persevere long enough to complete the stretch is to start thinking like a world champion athlete.

Dan served on the Olympic Committee for the 2002 Winter Games in Salt Lake City and witnessed firsthand the Olympic motto: "Citius, Altius, Fortius" (Faster, Higher, Stronger). Through individual and coached stretching, athletes from all over the world gathered in the belief that world records were made to be broken if they simply focused on bettering their own past best personal performance.

One such athlete's story illuminates the constant and direct interdependent connection between perseverance and stretching. The year was 1987, when U.S. speed skater Dan Jansen's sister Jane, who was also a speed skater, was diagnosed with leukemia. Inspired by her relentless battle to live, Dan won three gold medals at the World Championships held in Milwaukee just two weeks before the 1988 Calgary Olympic Games.

But seven hours before the biggest race of his career, Dan received word that his sweet sister had passed away. Despite his inconceivable sorrow, he resolved he would win for Jane, determined to live up to everyone's expectations and capture the gold.

Lining up for the 500-meter sprint against Japan's Yasushi Kuroiwa, Jansen adjusted the hood on his sleek racing suit and took a deep breath. Clearly his body was there but not his mind or his heart.

Of course, he busted out of the starting blocks, but in the first turn suddenly and shockingly fell and skidded violently into the padded wall — a heartbreaking scene of agony. With the world watching, he slowly rose from the ice and skated toward the side of the oval. Feeling he had let his sister down, he buried his face in his hands.

In the following 1000-meter race he fell again. In 1992, at Albertville, France, he placed fourth in the 500-meter and an embarrassing twenty-sixth in the 1000-meter. Despite these disappointments, Jansen continued to persevere and stretch himself in his training, retaining his place on the U.S. Olympic team for the 1994 games.

In the 500-meter race, he slipped momentarily, avoiding a fall but losing enough time to wind up in eighth place. In the 1000-meter race, his last Olympic event and his last race ever, Jansen finally won a gold medal, establishing a world-record time of 1 minute 12.43 seconds.

Jansen's coach, Dr. Jim Loehr, revealed that the reason Dan was finally able to win that elusive Olympic gold was that he had developed an emotional focus on the moment. Jim convinced Dan that thinking about winning for his sister, or dwelling on the fact that it was his last race and final opportunity to win an Olympic medal, was counterproductive and would drain his energy and detract from his focus.

All Jansen needed to do was to focus his stretch on "right now" and on each subsequent "right now," needing to persevere only one moment at a time. Technically, it was "one foot in front of the other." Mentally, it was to "maintain feelings of gratitude for all the years the sport had given him."

Persevering so we can stretch ourselves to our ultimate capacity and potential as human beings becomes simple (although not easy!) when we block out all distractions, avoid the "paralysis of analysis" of thinking too much, and focus all our concentrated energy and emotion on the "stretching" task at hand.

"Never Say Never"

Richard Nelson, a sixteen-year-old junior at Manti High School in Utah, was an outstanding athlete. He was the number-two singles player on the state championship tennis team and had just made the basketball team that would go on that year to win the state championship. He was looking forward to much success as a senior during the following season. But on October 23, 1966, most of his athletic future was suddenly taken away from him.

That night, Richard was riding his bicycle from Manti to Gunnison to visit his girlfriend. The road was very steep in some places, which allowed Richard to reach speeds of forty miles per hour on the downhill slopes. Because it was dark and difficult to see, Richard was following the white line on the shoulder of the road to ensure his safety. As he came around a blind curve and was looking down at the ground, Richard failed to see a parked car jacked up to fix a flat tire on his side of the road. With no warning, he hit the parked car and ended up in the hospital, where he didn't regain consciousness for two days.

Besides bad cuts on his head and knee, he broke his collarbone and right arm. He wore an L-shaped cast on his arm for two months. When the cast came off on December 29, Richard's doctor gave him a series of tests to determine the success of his healing. Richard failed all the tests. His triceps muscle had lost all its strength – he could not push out with his arm. The doctor diagnosed a pinched nerve and said that Richard might never regain the use of his right arm. Richard's once strong but now puny right arm just hung at his side, and the doctor gave him no real hope of recovery.

Because of his injury, Richard wasn't able to play on the basketball team during the rest of that year, but the coach made him equipment and statistics manager so that he could come to practice and be around the guys on the team. His junior year ended, the summer came, and Richard was determined to do whatever he had to do to make the basketball team the next year. He realized that he couldn't make it right-handed, so he started working on his left-handed skills.

All summer long, each and every night, he practiced making left-handed baskets at the outdoor courts in the center of town. Every night, he shot two hundred left-handed baskets and practiced left-handed dribbling and passing off the park retaining wall. Instead of going with his friends to the summer dances sponsored by the high school, Richard practiced basketball.

When the next season arrived, Richard was ready to try out for the team – and he made it! He never became a starter but he was always the first substitute to go in the game. The season boiled down to the final game of the year against their archrival, Richfield High. This game would determine which team would win the league championship and advance to the state tournament playoffs. It was a "must win" for both teams.

On Friday night, the gym was packed. The starting guard for Manti had sprained his ankle earlier in the week, so Richard finally got his big break – he started the game! However, before the first quarter was over, Richard was replaced. It was hard to compete when he could only use one arm. The game continued until the last thirty seconds when Manti's other guard was injured, forcing Richard back into the game. Richfield was ahead by three points, and Manti had the ball.

The Richfield team's coach tried to take advantage of the situation by having one of his players immediately foul Richard. Undaunted, Richard stepped up to the free throw line. (If he made the first foul shot, he would get a chance to shoot and make a second basket.) Confidently, Richard picked up the ball, braced it in his left hand, and shot. Swish! He made it, and the crowd went wild! He then made the next shot, bringing Manti High to within one point of Richfield. The crowd stood and went crazy again!

Richfield then took the ball out of bounds and threw a long pass down court to the player Richard was guarding, trying to make a quick, easy basket. But Richard, with his undying determination, leaped through the air to intercept the pass. When he landed he was fouled again, and was given another opportunity at the free throw line. With ten seconds left on the clock, Richard balanced the ball in his left hand, took a deep breath, and shot. The crowd was deathly quiet until – swish! He tied the game! His next shot went up, down and through. Swish again!

He made it – he made all four shots – left-handed! Richard Nelson won the game and became the hero of the school. According to Richard Nelson, he was not a hero. "Anybody could have done what I did," he said in his postgame interview. "I was supposed to make those shots. Everybody was counting on me to win the game when I was put in that situation. All I did was believe in myself, work hard when others didn't, and persevere.

Anybody could have done what I did in the game if they had shot as many foul shots as I had shot last summer in practice." As Earl Nightingale said, "The only difference between a successful person and an unsuccessful person is that the successful person will do what the unsuccessful person will not do. The key is the successful person does not want to do it either, but then does it anyway."

"It's Not Over 'Til It's Over"

The 2007 NCAA BCS Fiesta Bowl will go down as one of the greatest games and college bowls of all time. It had the David verses Goliath aspect with WAC Champion Boise State – undefeated at 12-0 and ranked 8th in the country, who have a phenomenal program having won 85 games in the last eight years with a blowout win over the same Oregon State team that beat USC this year, and decisive wins over Hawaii, Utah, and San Jose State who all won their bowl games – playing against 6th ranked Big Twelve Champion Oklahoma.

With 8 minutes left in the game Boise State was ahead 28-10. Then Oklahoma mounted a gut-check comeback including a two-point conversion attempt that required three tries before Sooners quarterback Paul Thompson was finally able to get the job done. Then there was the "they can't really lose like that can they?" interception thrown by Boise State quarterback Jared Zabransky for an Oklahoma touchdown on the first play from scrimmage after the Sooners tied it.

Then, with just over three minutes to play there was the epic Boise State 75-yard drive to tie the score back up to force overtime, which featured a 4th and 18-yard hook-and- ladder play for a touchdown with only 30 seconds left in the game. In overtime, Boise elected to be on defense first and on the first play, Oklahoma superstar running back Adrian Peterson, in what was likely his final carry of his college career, scampered for a 25-yard touchdown.

Now Boise State had to score a touchdown or they would lose. On 4th and 2 they made a tough first down. Then in a well-rehearsed gimmick play that sent the quarterback in motion, the back rolled right and threw a short touchdown pass. Boise is now behind by one point 42-41.

Would they just kick the extra point to tie it up and force a second overtime, or put it all on the line and go for two, knowing if they missed they would lose the hard fought game and ruin a perfect undefeated season? What would you have done? Boise State went for it, and with another perfectly executed coup de grace "statue-of-liberty" play they scored the two-point conversion to win 43-42. Unbelievable!

Say whatever you want about the New England Patriots. You love them. You hate them. But no matter where you come down on New England, give the Patriots this: over the past 15 years, they've entertained hundreds of millions of Americans on Super Bowl Sunday. They've made Super Bowl an even bigger spectacle, which is a pretty tough task. They do Super Bowls right.

All but one of the seven Tom Brady—Bill Belichick Super Bowls this century was decided in the final minute. The team's first win, in 2002, came on a field goal as time expired; the second, in 2004, came on a field goal with 4 seconds left. A last-second interception won the fourth; on Sunday the Pats clinched the fifth, the greatest comeback in Super Bowl history, on a walk-off touchdown in overtime, the first ever extra session in a Super Bowl.

New England's 34-28 victory over the Atlanta Falcons in Super Bowl LI Sunday night settled more than a few debates. No team had ever won a Super Bowl when trailing by more than 10 points. The Pats were down 28-3 with 8:31 left in the third quarter. And then New England scored 31 unanswered points to stun the Falcons.

Brady won his fifth Super Bowl; he's now the first starting QB to have earned that many titles. He set new records for most passes completed (43) and most passing yards (466) in Super Bowl history. He won his fourth MVP, another record. He's the best ever, full stop. Same for Belichick, the first head coach to win five Super Bowls.

On a first down with 2:28 left and the Pats down 28-20, Brady threw a pass to Julian Edelman over the middle of the field. Atlanta cornerback Robert Alford leapt and tapped the ball up in the air, two other Falcons, Ricardo Allen and Jalen Collins, converged on Edelman. He was utterly outnumbered.

The ball, however, somehow stuck on Alford's foot as he fell back, giving Edelman a split second to squeeze possession of the ball before it fell to the ground, and before Allen and Keanu Neal could get their hands on it. After that dazzling 23-yard pass play, Brady continued to cut the Falcons with short, surgical passes; from the one-yard-line, James White ran for a touchdown to complete a 10-play, 91-yard drive, one of the best of Brady's career. That's saying something.

With New England now trailing 28- 26, Danny Amendola took a Brady screen pass and punched the ball in the end zone to complete the two-point conversion, and tie the game at 28. At that point, not even the most loyal Falcon fan could doubt the Pats would win the game. New England just couldn't stop scoring. The Pats won the overtime coin toss, and put together an efficient 75 -yard drive, capped off by White's 2-yard touchdown run to clinch it and again win the Super Bowl!

"Playing To Win Or Not To Lose"

What's the point? Teams that are ahead at halftime face a decision. Either they keep fighting and playing to win, or they stop taking risks, try to live off their past success, and start playing not to lose.

Playing not to lose is when we stop our aggressive offense and replace it with defensive carefulness, when we lose that eye-of-the-tiger intensity that gave us the competitive advantage in the first place, when our fear of risk and failure outweighs our desire to succeed.

In business, if you are failing or losing market share, you don't fall apart, lose focus, and give up. And if you're doing well, capturing market share and making more money than you imagined, you don't get cocky and complacent. Whether you are ahead or behind, you must take charge and press on!

An example of everything we've discussed actually took place in one form or another in the single year of 1985. In only his fourth year in the NFL, quarterback Jim McMahon led his Chicago Bears to the Super Bowl World Championship; Ed Pickney, weakened by the flu, played the game of his life against Georgetown's Patrick Ewing as underdog Villanova won the

NCAA basketball championship; little-known Danny Sullivan spun his race car 360 degrees going 200 miles an hour, and seconds later won the Indianapolis 500 in dramatic fashion; a slow running, 44-year-old, gray-haired pro baseball player with no exceptional talent named Pete Rose broke Ty Cobb's all-time base- hit record of 4,191; and pro baseball pitcher Phil Niekro won his 300th game at the age of 50.

Never say never! And if you're the right person, in the right circumstances, it's never too late. Ever.

CLOSING TRIBUTE TO EVERY COACH WHO EVER LIVED!

QUIET HEROES

The world is full of quiet heroes who never seek
the praise,
They're always back off in the shadows,
They let us have the limelight days.

For this you're the one that I look up to, Because
of you I'm free,
You set an example I could follow,
You helped me see my destiny.

So even though my thanks don't show,
Unnoticed you will never go,
I need to say I love you so,
You're my hero.

I've had my share of broken dreams,
But you said I could win.
You gave me the chance I always needed to start
my dreams again.

You took the time to teach and tutor and show me
rules to rise,
You changed my fears to glory tears,
You're an angel in disguise.

Unless you coached me through the maze and
I wouldn't be where I am today, I've won my share
of times, pushed me on the hardest climbs.
It's just your style, the extra mile, no glory must be
tough,
You let me have the accolades,
A smile, you said, was just enough.

So even though my thanks don't show,
Unnoticed you will never go,
I need to say I love you so,
You're my hero.
© Dan Clark 1983

OTHER BOOKS BY DAN CLARK

The Art of Significance
-Achieving The Level Beyond Success
(Audiobook Also Available)

The Art of Significance Workbook
Study Guide / Training Manual

The Art of Significant Relationships
- Anthology Of Fifteen Experts

The Art of Raising Significant Children

The Art of Significant Leadership
- How to Grow People Into Passionate Partners

The Art of Significant Selling
- How To Get People To Choose You Instead Of Just
Somebody Who Does What You Do

The Art of Significant Team Building
- Where Self-Mastery is Permanent, Winning is Personal
and High Performance is Automatic

The Art of Significant Speaking and Storytelling
- What I Learned From Zig Ziglar That You Should Know

The Art of Significant Network Marketing
(Audiobook and Study Guide)

Chicken Soup for the College Soul

The Most Popular Stories By Dan Clark In

Chicken Soup For The Soul

Puppies for Sale
(Illustrated Children's Hard Cover Storybook)

Soul Food
(The Complete Dan Clark Story Collection)

Puppies for Sale and Other Inspirational Tales

Dan Clark's Humor File
—   A Repository of Jokes and B.S. Tales

The Treasury of Dan Clark Quotes, Lyrics and Poems

TO CONTACT DAN
for a Keynote Speech, and/or to conduct a 1 to 3 day
Training:

1-8oo-676-1121

Website: danclark.com

Email: dan@danclark.com